W9-BBH-364

Uneven Land

STEPHANIE L. SARVER

Uneven Land

Nature and Agriculture in American Writing

UNIVERSITY OF NEBRASKA PRESS *Lincoln and London*

© 1999 by the University of Nebraska Press

All rights reserved

Manufactured in the United States of America

☉

Library of Congress Cataloging-in-Publication Data

Sarver, Stephanie L., 1955–

Uneven land : nature and agriculture in American

writing / Stephanie Sarver.

p.   cm.

Includes bibliographical references

(p.   ) and index.

ISBN 0-8032-4252-2 (cloth: alk. paper)

1. American literature—History and criticism.

2. Nature in literature.   3. Pastoral literature,

American—History and criticism.   4. Country life

in literature.   5. Agriculture in literature.

6. Landscape in literature.   7. Farm life in

literature.   8. Land use in literature.   I. Title.

PS163.S27   1999

810.9′36—dc21   99-17853

CIP

for Selma Hendrickson and Elsie Hendrickson

CONTENTS

❦ ❦ ❦

ACKNOWLEDGMENTS

MANY PEOPLE have assisted me in this project. I am indebted to David Robertson for his careful reading and criticism of *Uneven Land* and for his introducing me to those affiliated with the Program in Nature and Culture at the University of California at Davis. Jack Hicks, Scott McLean, Gary Snyder, Lenora Timm, Mark Wheelis, and David Wilson offered me valuable guidance. David Van Leer, Margit Stange, James Marois, Sean O'Grady, Mark Hoyer, and Mary Edmonds earn special thanks for reading this work at various stages and returning helpful comments. Christine King lent assistance through her impressive knowledge of Frank Norris. Harold Glasser answered numerous questions about environmental philosophy and ethics and critiqued my work. Tom Harris, Joe Mills, Michael Marchetti, Maryann Owens, Kate Reavey, Trina Schimmoeller, Eric Todd Smith, and Christopher Sindt gave their time for discussions about agriculture, wilderness, and life. Michael Krasny has been a mentor and friend. Marilyn Chandler McEntyre and Thomas Strychacz encouraged my raw thoughts on environmentalism and agriculture in their classes at Mills College. Those thoughts became this book.

Lawrence B. Lee, George Sessions, and Peter Wild provided me with new leads when my own searches had led me down blind alleys. Michael Branch shared his work on Emerson, and David Teague offered me helpful direction in my work on Smythe. David Robinson shared his work on Crèvecoeur; he and Susan Rosowski provided suggestions for the revision of this book.

An early version of my chapter on Smythe appeared in *Western American Literature*; Thomas Lyon offered helpful editorial direction. A condensation of my discussion on Emerson appears in

Reading the Earth: New Directions in the Study of Literature and Environment (Moscow: U of Idaho P, 1998), edited by Michael P. Branch.

Thanks to my parents, who believed that their urban children should know something about farm life. Our visits to the Scaroni ranch north of Santa Cruz and to the Aalto farm in Reedley, California, introduced me to the forms of nature that reside in agrarian lands. And thanks to Tom Barclay and Abbie Havens, who offered me much support as I wrote this.

Finally, I wish to acknowledge the Davis school, whose unique influence has infused every page of this book.

ABBREVIATIONS

AT	Liberty Hyde Bailey, *Apple-Tree*
CAA	William Ellsworth Smythe, *Conquest of Arid America*, 1905
CW	Ralph Waldo Emerson, *Collected Works*
EFS	Ralph Waldo Emerson, *Essays: First and Second Series*
EL	Ralph Waldo Emerson, *Early Lectures*
JMN	Ralph Waldo Emerson, *Journals and Miscellaneous Notebooks*
MTR	Hamlin Garland, *Main-Travelled Roads*
NSI	Liberty Hyde Bailey, *Nature-Study Idea*
OMTR	Hamlin Garland, *Other Main-Travelled Roads*
RI	William Ellsworth Smythe, "Republic of Irrigation."
W	Ralph Waldo Emerson, *Complete Works*

Uneven Land

Introduction

I BEGIN this work by reflecting not on agriculture and nature but on libraries. One afternoon as I wandered through the Shields Library at the University of California at Davis, I realized the logic of my larger method. I found myself following a circuit through the library stacks that I had repeated countless times over the several years during which I wrote this book. Climbing the great stairs from the library lobby, I wended my way to the southwest corner of the second floor. I arrived at the section containing books concerned with ecology and environmental philosophy. My eyes ran across titles I had come to know well. I found books about environmental ethics, the science of ecology, and the philosophies of deep ecology, social ecology, and ecofeminism. I found books examining how we have altered the earth and how we can protect our planet from human ravages.

From there I moved east, into the old south wing of the library to the collection pertaining to public policy. Down a row of dark aisles I found volumes on agricultural economics and the business of farming. The titles here suggested a perpetual crisis in agriculture, predicting economic doom for farmers resulting from two centuries of misguided government policies. I climbed a flight of stairs to the third floor. There in the east wing I found a great

1

room filled with books on agricultural history, agronomy, farm management, and agricultural practice. The titles of the books here revealed a calmer tone, seeming to reflect the steady head of scientific objectivity. These volumes prescribed farming practices and tendered practical advice founded on scientific observation. This section contained the books written by people who worked the land, either as scientific agrarians or as actual farmers. Some books considered the social and personal dimensions of farming, suggesting how individuals find meaning in the agrarian way of life. Among these volumes I found works authored by Liberty Hyde Bailey explaining the science of horticulture and the philosophy of farming.

I climbed still another flight of stairs to the north wing of the library. Here were the books of and about American literature. Buried on the shelves I found the crafted prose, the literature, of Ralph Waldo Emerson, Hamlin Garland, Frank Norris, and Bailey. In these volumes, farming figured not as a subject but as a context to human experiences rendered in essay and fiction. As I stood in this room, I was aware that tucked on a shelf directly on the floor below, in a section devoted to the history of irrigation, was a book by William Ellsworth Smythe that documented water politics in California. I recalled that scattered throughout the library, in unexpected places, I would find the agricultural texts of Cato the Elder, Xenophon, Virgil, François Quesnay, Thomas Jefferson, and Wendell Berry.

My path through the library reflects the odd way we categorize thought. I write about agriculture, yet the books I use in my work are scattered throughout the library—a situation indicating that if one were confined to a single section, a single branch of thought, one's understanding of agriculture would be circumscribed, distorted, and incomplete. The clustered communities of agrarian books suggest a fact of agriculture that underscores this book: it is an activity entangled in manifold aspects of American life and thought. Agriculture figures in our physical well-being, in our economy, in our national identity, in the transformation of the earth, and the loss of biological diversity. For many who practice it, farming represents a spiritual connection to the earth.

Because of the myriad dimensions of agriculture, the farm has become a repository for a range of beliefs and the metaphoric vehicle through which many people explore their relationship with or place in nature. For some Americans the farm is the seat of Jefferson's agrarian democracy; for African Americans it may figure as the seat of exploitation and oppression. The farm is the place where a naturalist such as Henry David Thoreau could explore his spirituality and where utopian visionaries such as George Ripley could create an ideal society. With the closing of the American frontier a century ago, the farm has gradually become the figurative ground where the archetypal little guy dukes it out with larger oppressive forces. The agrarian literature of the past century, from Hamlin Garland to John Steinbeck to Jane Smiley, reveals the economic tensions that increasingly characterize farming as it is practiced in the United States.[1]

In the past two decades, some environmental philosophers have identified the farm as the site of the fall from late-Paleolithic grace. Contemporaneous with that interpretation of the farm, a new breed of agrarians has emerged, exemplified by Wendell Berry and Wes Jackson, who regard the farm as a site where community may be regenerated through a reverent stewardship of the land. Indeed, as the farm reflects the convergence of these multiple threads of thought, it also figures as the place where arguments about the impact of humans on the environment converge.

Uneven Land attempts to decipher the relationship between humans and nature as it appears in discussions of agriculture. I focus on Ralph Waldo Emerson, Frank Norris, William Ellsworth Smythe, Hamlin Garland, and Liberty Hyde Bailey because they document a period of agricultural transformation, when the nation, fueled by collective myths surrounding the importance of the small farm, expanded into the lands west of the Mississippi River. The period from 1860 to 1920 was significant as one during which agriculture was transformed by technology and by the diminishing availability of inexpensive arable land. Railroads made possible the shipment of agricultural products over great distances, while advances in farming and irrigation technology encouraged the wholesale transformation of Midwestern prairie and Southwestern desert into farmland. Concurrently, the arable Western lands, which had provided the national imagination with an arena for unlimited growth, were absorbed into private ownership. The five writers that I consider reflect these changes, simultaneously embracing new agricultural realities while resisting and sometimes mourning the loss of an earlier agrarian way that allowed for a more intimate experience of nature.

Women writing during this period were hardly silent on their own experiences of nature, but their texts generally center in gardening, nature study, and ranching.[2] While the issues that these women address reflect their roles within a particular social and domestic sphere in the era that I consider here, their writings do not dramatically illustrate the specific tensions that I examine. In addition, because the issues surrounding agriculture as it has been experienced by displaced and marginalized communities are deserving of attention beyond the scope of such a study as this, I have limited my focus to works by American authors of Anglo-European descent. I hope my discussion of these five writers encourages other scholars to explore how agrarian nature is depicted in the texts of a much broader range of writers.

Agriculture has occupied an ambiguous conceptual position in American thought, belonging both to a green world of nature, a realm that exists independent of human control, and to a world defined by a human culture that dominates and influences nature. The five writers on whom I focus may be regarded as nodes on a continuum of agrarian and American writing, a continuum reaching back to the ancient texts of such writers as Hesiod, Cato, and Virgil and to the relatively recent American texts written by Thomas Jefferson and Hector St. John de Crèvecoeur. The writers I examine have been succeeded by others—such as Willa Cather, John Steinbeck, Louis Bromfield, and Wendell Berry—who have translated their concerns about agriculture into a range of fiction and nonfiction texts.[3]

I situate this work within a movement in literary criticism that considers how literature depicts human relationships with non-human environments. Scholars of literature have long considered this relationship, but their interpretations have been limited by an anthropocentric tendency to interpret environment primarily as the human milieu defining human existence. When scholars consider depictions of nature in literature, they are often concerned with nature as envisioned within the Enlightenment or romantic intellectual traditions, more interested in the history of thought than with how such thought may influence human behavior as it affects the environment. When nonhuman environments are pulled into analyses of literature, they are seen only as the stages on which human dramas are enacted or the raw materials that make possible human progress.

In recent decades literary scholars have become more attuned to the nonhuman environment as an entity that not only influences humans but which humans also influence. In 1972 in *The Comedy of Survival* Joseph Meeker introduced the concept of "literary ecology" and explored "the possible correspondences between the cultural creations of mankind, especially literature, and the requirements of a balanced natural ecology" (xx). He considered how classic literary modes have influenced the worldview of centuries of Westerners to adopt behaviors that often carry negative environmental consequences. The tragic mode, which is distinctly Western, has encouraged a worldview that defines human success as an ability to overcome and to dominate one's environment. Conversely the comic mode, which is also apparent in non-Western cultures, reveals humans successfully adapting to environmental influences. Meeker explicitly positions his book within the context of modern environmentalism in an attempt to make relevant his study of ancient literary traditions. A few years later Annette Kolodny brought an ecological and feminist perspective to a study of American literature in *The Lay of the Land*. She addressed America's "most cherished fantasy" of a harmonious relationship with a feminine pastoral land, asserting that the American pastoral fantasy is driven by a dominant metaphor that emphasizes a "regression from the cares of adult life and a return to the primal warmth of womb or breast in a feminine landscape" (6). Like Meeker, Kolodny openly invoked a larger environmentalist context as she argued that the values of our culture as they relate to the environment are embedded in the texts created by generations of writers. Contemporaneous with Kolodony and Meeker, William Rueckert suggested in "Literature and Ecology: An Experiment in Ecocriticism" that a "principle of relevance" (73) be brought to literary criticism. He challenged the tendency of literary scholars "to produce theories which are evermore elegant, more baroque, more scholastic" (74) as they emphasize newness over relevance to a larger world. His experiment with literary ecology is now more often invoked for his coining of the term "ecocriticism" than for his speculative efforts to view poetry through an ecological lens.

✓ The late 1980s brought a refreshed attention to environmental issues and literary study as scholars turned to nature writing—texts that had hitherto been regarded as outside of the literary canon. Many embraced Thoreau as an exemplary naturalist who revealed an ecological sensibility in his close observations of the New England land he traveled and inhabited. Several scholars expanded the definitions of literature by turning to such writers as John Muir and Mary Austin, authors who previously had been ignored as subjects of scholarly scrutiny. Throughout the early 1990s scholars linked the study of wilderness texts with an environmentalist awareness.[4] Glen Love suggests that for many "wild nature has replaced the traditional middle state of the garden and the rural landscape as the locus of stability and value" (203). Indeed, as literature scholars have directed their attention to nature writing and texts that take as their focus nonhuman nature, they have elevated wilderness to an exalted position. Yet their focus on wilderness has left another realm—land more visibly transformed by human hands—unscrutinized.

While one group of scholars has considered how writers interpret their experiences of wilderness, others have considered American nature writing as the continuation of a lengthy pastoral tradition. Studies of American literature often fold agrarian literature into that tradition, regarding farmland as a realm idealized by an urban citizenry as an antidote to urban life. Indeed, that pastoral sensibility is evident in the work of Emerson as well as Thoreau, who openly treated his agrarian experiment at Walden as a challenge to the prevailing values of his era. Hamlin Garland and Liberty Bailey may also be interpreted as yearning for farm life as a balm for the pains of civilization. I do not, however, focus on their work as reflecting a pastoral sensibility—which, at heart, abstracts agrarian land into an imaginative space. Some regard the pastoral as an impulse to "return" to a natural world; for some this natural world is wild nature. A pastoral interpretation of literature may be too restrictive in analyzing agrarian literature. Indeed, I focus on agriculture as a ground whereon the forces of urban civilization meet the forces of unmediated nature, but I consider this middle space not only as an imaginative but as an actual space wherein occur actual events that have terrestrial consequences.

Uneven Land is also influenced by larger movements within environmental philosophy and ethics. Environmentalists may classify agriculture as a product of civilization and its institutions; conversely, popular culture often regards agriculture as an adjunct of nature. Scholars who have studied agricultural texts have generally foregrounded political and social issues while marginalizing the significance of nature itself. The texts that consider agriculture often reveal the interplay of nonhuman nature and human culture; thus they provide an ideal ground for examining not only how humans relate to nature but also how their political, social, and economic institutions influence the way they impact the land they inhabit.

The debates surrounding agriculture and environmental philosophy often hinge on questions surrounding the concept of nature. The most vocal critics of modern agriculture have identified the emergence of cultivation as the moment that marks the decline of humanity. Environmental philosophers such as Paul Shepard and Max Oelschlaeger argue that prior to the rise of agriculture, humans lived as hunter-gatherers, surviving in ways that did not disturb a larger balance of nature.[5] Implicit in their view is the assumption that the relationship between all humans and all other biological entities was somehow static prior to the Neolithic era, that nature operated according to an order in which no species exerted a pressure on another that seriously altered the other's place in a larger balanced state. The view of these environmental philosophers regards humans as natural animals only if they rely on hunting and foraging for their sustenance.

Critics of agriculture argue that the cultivation of plants for food represents a larger problem with regard to human perception. Many contend that agriculture evolved from a worldview that emphasized the proliferation of humans at the expense of other species and of the integrity of the larger environment. Deep ecologists such as Arne Naess and George Sessions identify this worldview as anthropocentrism and define it as a perceptual system that places humans at the apex of an hierarchical order.[6] Lynn White Jr. argues that anthropocentric views of nature are encouraged by the Judeo-Christian tradition, which charges humans with dominion over nonhuman nature, while David Ehrenfeld condemns humanism for its role in promoting a belief that human ingenuity can resolve all environmental problems through technology. An anthropocentric worldview, with its concomitant domination of nature, often is identified as the root cause of environmental problems.[7] An attitude of domination over nature encourages its exploitation. When nature is intellectually reduced to a commodity existing only for the benefit of humans, many argue, its degradation and destruction easily follow.

Gary Snyder looks to the concept of wildness as the important factor in shaping human perception and behavior.[8] He argues that humans can retain their inherently animal qualities if they retain their wildness; thus by living closer to an unmanipulated nature— that is, a nature not transformed by human hands—primitive peoples are more attuned to a natural order than are modern urban people. Snyder encourages a distinction between wild and domesticated rather than natural and unnatural, observing that "New York City and Tokyo are 'natural'" as part of the larger physical universe but are hardly wild (8–10). He suggests that humans would exist in greater harmony with all of creation if we would recover the wildness that was characteristic of late-Paleolithic humans. Implicit in Snyder's view is a criticism of agriculture, which represents domestication, a process that is antithetical to wildness.[9]

I am less concerned with determining whether a behavior or perception is inherently natural or unnatural, wild or domesticated, than I am with identifying the ways that such perceptions figure in our relationships with agrarian land. Within this larger work, I assume that humans are a part of nature and that even our agriculture is inherently natural as an expression of our efforts to survive. At issue is not whether agriculture is bad or good but how agriculture figures in our experience and in our earthly existence. I do not dispute the impact of human agriculture in transforming the planet. Nevertheless, I do wish to consider how agriculture has figured in our thinking and how its practice, which is both economic and social, requires a relationship with nonhuman nature that is simultaneously material and spiritual.

Nature is a concept packed with manifold meanings and implications. It is a slippery idea and an even more slippery word. Emerson attempted to clarify the various meanings of *nature* when he commenced his discussion on the subject in 1836, suggesting that nature might be defined in both its common and its philosophical senses. Common nature included those entities untouched by man; the philosophical sense was more inclusive and embraced all that is "not me," including the human body. John Stuart Mill grappled with similar concepts two decades later when he suggested that "The word Nature has two principal meanings: it either denotes the entire system of things, with the aggregate of all their properties, or it denotes things as they would be, apart from human intervention" (341).

Over a century later we are still explaining what we mean by the term. Gary Snyder acknowledges the duality of *nature*, defining the term as meaning "'the out-doors'—the physical world, including all living things. Nature by this definition is a norm of the world that is apart from the features or products of civilization and human will. . . . The other meaning, which is broader, is 'the material world and its collective objects and phenomena,' including the products of human action and intention" (8). We continue to circle over the same ground, recognizing that we can regard nature as both a quality and a terrestrial entity. Neil Evernden, who distinguishes between the objects we assign to the category "nature" and the concept of nature, sets his discussion within the context of cultural and philosophical studies and proposes that nature is both "actual" and "cultural" (xi), that it is both a material reality and a culturally determined concept.

In writing *Uneven Land* I have concluded that semantic precision is impossible. Even as I have consciously attempted to anchor my use of the term *nature*, I have found that its manifold meanings and associations sometimes elude me. I have, however, attempted to employ certain definitions in my discussion: generally, when I speak of nature, I refer to entities exclusive of humans, particularly to biological entities such as insects, birds, animals, plants, and the environments in which they exist. In certain moments, when I am considering the ways that humans figure as natural entities, I may refer to "nonhuman nature" to distinguish the human animal from other natural entities. When discussing nature as an amorphous force, I attempt to anchor those discussions within that larger concept, particularly as I consider Emerson and Norris. The ambiguities surrounding my use of these terms reflect the ambiguities inherent in the texts I consider.

THOSE ACCUSTOMED to reading traditional books of literary scholarship will expect that I provide some historical context, indeed, some literary context to this larger work. As a nod to my editor (a historian himself) I will briefly consider the eighteenth century. Thomas Jefferson and St. Jean de Crèvecoeur figure as "the usual suspects" in any discussion of American agricultural writing because they provide us with an early national expression of an American agrarian sensibility. Their work exhibits a tension that defines farming and that will be evident a century or more

later in the writers who are the focus of this book. Both describe ✓
farming as an activity that provides to its practitioner a beneficial
experience of nature. This activity simultaneously figures within
the political and economic webs of the society in which it is
practiced. Moreover, both Jefferson and Crèvecoeur reveal in their
work an awareness that agriculture, even in their era, transformed
the land in ways that were sometimes detrimental to the agrarian
enterprise. They invoke remarkably similar themes, not because
they were in deep psychic harmony but because they wrote to the
issues that were a part of the larger discourse of their era.

Thomas Jefferson merits a brief mention for his role in establishing the importance of the small farm in our society and for
contributing to the creation of the yeoman farmer as a national
archetype. Discussions of agriculture in American life frequently
invoke the expression "Jeffersonian agrarianism," a term that describes a complex of values that emerged from the late eighteenth
century. Jefferson believed that farmers were the mainstay of a
sound economy and social order. In his vision, the farm would
form the basic unit around which an agrarian democracy would
be organized. As a student of the Enlightenment, Jefferson embraced property ownership as a fundamental human right; thus
he worked to ensure that the constitutional foundation of the new
nation would facilitate and encourage land ownership among a
diverse population. His ideas gained greater weight as the United
States expanded into the lands west of the Mississippi River. The
Homestead Act of 1862, which granted 160 acres to any citizen, is
regarded as a fulfillment of this agrarian vision. Jefferson contributed in a central way to the formation of a collective value—some
might argue, a myth—of a nation of freeholder farmers, average
men who figure as the cornerstone of democracy. This agrarian
myth figures as a subtext to the works I consider in this study.

Jefferson's "Notes on the State of Virginia" is often cited as a
moment when he asserts his belief in the farm as the unit around
which a democracy should be organized. Query 19 has become a ✓
set piece for illustrating Jefferson's views of agriculture, a moment
when he declares that farmers are central to a sound democracy.

He wrote: "Those who labour in the earth are the chosen people of God, if ever he had a chosen people, whose breasts he has made his peculiar deposit for substantial and genuine virtue" ("Notes" 290). Jefferson argues that democracy is best supported by a diverse land-holding population who are of an inherently high moral character through their close association with the earth. Although Jefferson addresses the issue of social order, his emphasis on farming as a source of human virtue is derived from an underlying belief that an intimate relationship with nonhuman nature is beneficial to the individual.[10]

Jefferson was himself a farmer. His understanding of agriculture is evident throughout his personal letters, in which he discusses not just democracy but also such mundane topics as crop rotation and manuring. The land Jefferson farmed had a lengthy agricultural history. Even in his era, the farmlands of Virginia and the greater colonies were facing declining fertility and topsoil loss through farming practices that did little to sustain the land. Albemarle County, where much of Jefferson's land was seated, had a long history of agricultural mismanagement that had resulted in soil erosion (see McEwan 1–19). He was aware that agriculture and other land practices resulted in negative environmental consequences, and he supported land surveys that would document the effects of deforestation on climate.[11]

Jefferson understood that a knowledgeable farmer also should be a student of natural history and versed in such sciences as horticulture and agronomy. Such knowledge, Jefferson felt, would enhance a farmer's appreciation for the natural processes intrinsic to the practice of agriculture. Jefferson's values will continue to reappear through the agrarian literature of the next centuries. They will be evident in Emerson, who transforms the Jeffersonian vision into his own brand of transcendental agrarianism. They will also be visible in the work of Hamlin Garland as he laments the failure of an agrarian democracy in his attack on land speculators who have corrupted the spirit of Jefferson's vision. And these values will appear in the work of William Smythe, who asserts the enduring potential Jefferson's dream through reconfiguration of arid Western lands.

St. John de Crèvecoeur brought a somewhat quirkier vision of agriculture to his reflections on colonial life in both *Letters from an American Farmer* and *Sketches of Eighteenth-Century America.* Crèvecoeur, born in France to a family of petty nobility, settled around 1770 in Orange County, New Jersey, where he purchased the two hundred fifty acres that he farmed until the Revolution.[12] He is best known for his efforts to define the American character in his *Letters* (published in 1782). His work also speaks to the imaginative place of farmers in American thought. He describes farmers as naturalists—as men who derive satisfaction from their work, in part, through its intimate association with nonhuman nature. While Jefferson is relevant to this discussion for the way that he helped to codify certain agrarian ideals, Crèvecoeur figures ✓ as a literary forefather to my eclectic cluster of writers because he acknowledges, perhaps inadvertently, that farming is simultaneously as political and social as it is personal and spiritual.

Like Jefferson, Crèvecoeur links the special experience of the farmer not only to his privileged relationships with nature but also to the experience of working land that he owns. In *Letters* he emphasizes the joys of farming and the blessings of a nation that allows the farmer the freedom to own land. However, he tempers the joyful experience of land ownership in his later *Sketches.*[13] There he considers the debt burdens facing colonial farmers— who are "obliged to borrow" at the risk of long-term debt—and addresses a theme that will persist in the work of Hamlin Garland and Frank Norris (273). Crèvecoeur injects a serious dimension to farming as he acknowledges the economic realities that influence its practice.

Crèvecoeur also describes the rich intangible benefits that accrue to the farmer's experience as a result of his intimate relationship with nature. In the *Letters* and *Sketches* Crèvecoeur develops a view of farming that affirms the natural bounty that defined the colonial farmland. The farmer is the privileged witness of "the sweet love tales of our robins" and the "sublime accents of the thrush from on high" (*Letters* 61). The farmer would also do well to know natural history, for such knowledge will impart an understanding of ecological balance—a condition not yet named in Crèvecoeur's era but one he nonetheless understood. In letter 2 he describes the life cycle of bees and kingbirds and tells us how their various feeding habits influence his farm: "I am astonished to see that nothing exists but what has its enemy; one species pursues and lives upon the other" (*Letters* 55). Crèvecoeur returns to this phenomenon in the *Sketches* when he observes: "If Nature has formed mice, she has created also the fox and the owl. They both prey on these. Were it not for their kind assistance, [the mice] would drive us out of our farms" (297). Crèvecoeur understands that humans survive within the "astonishing equipoise" of a larger nature, and he applies this understanding to higher philosophical questions when he considers the natural rights of the creatures of his farm. He ponders the blackbirds that plague his fields, asking "are they not the children of the great Creator as well as we?" (293–94). In posing such a question about natural rights, Crèvecoeur may figure as a forerunner to the ecocentric views that will emerge in later nineteenth-century writers such as Liberty Hyde Bailey.

Crèvecoeur also anticipates the writers I consider here when he acknowledges the impact of agriculture on colonial lands. In *Letters from an American Farmer* he creates an imaginative encounter with the famous botanist John Bartram, who came to his calling in botany while plowing a field. Bartram reflects: " 'What a shame,' said my mind . . . 'that thee shouldest have employed so many years in tilling the earth and destroying so many flowers and plants without being acquainted with their structures and their uses!' " (194). "Mr. Bertram" describes his own organic farming techniques, which include crop rotations of nitrogen-fixing clover and applications of a "good coat of mud," green fertilizer gleaned from a compost derived from "old lime, ashes, horse dung, . . . old hay, straw, and whatever damaged fodder" he has about his barn (192–93). In this mindful union of modern agronomy and natural history, Bartram is an enlightened agrarian, a man who can enjoy a higher intellectual relationship with his land while nonetheless working it for his own economic well-being.

If Crèvecoeur's colonial America is a land blessed with happy farmers, it is also a land that reveals the effects of agricultural mismanagement. He lauds Bartram's farm, which had once been "putrid swampy soil, useless either for the plough or for the scythe" (*Letters* 190). We may assume that Bartram's wetland provided a habitat for a few waterfowl before it was "rescued from the Schuylkill" (190) by dikes and drainage to create a prosperous, sustainable farm. Crèvecoeur is not so congratulatory to the farmer who practices an ignorant and shortsighted agriculture that exhausts the land, rendering it unsuitable for future agriculture. In *Sketches of Eighteenth-Century America* he compares the lands of the Tidewater region with the "Northern provinces," observing that the "fecundity of the earth is greatly diminished" where the topsoil has been lost (354). He also comments on a consequence of deforestation and swamp draining, which have reduced "to almost nothing" the streams and brooks that had once powered grist mills (285). Crèvecoeur acknowledges that certain kinds of agrarian practices can result in sustainable farming, while others may result in a depletion of resources that cannot be corrected. In contemplating the loss of brooks and streams as a consequence of deforestation he asks, "Who knows how far these effects may extend?" (285). The solution that seems obvious to Crèvecoeur is merely to move west. He quietly segues from observations on the impoverished condition of New England farmland to the promisingly fertile lands yet undeveloped in the wilderness of the Susquehanna.

Crèvecoeur invokes a theme that will run through American literature as he laments changes wrought by human progress as he simultaneously lauds them. While recognizing the irrevocable alterations to the land imposed by farming, he offers little by way of commentary for intervention; instead, he looks to the far west as the great hope, thereby affirming the expectation that will become characteristically American: exhaust the soil and move on. Crèvecoeur acknowledges the limitations facing the farmer, who despite his best efforts at working with nature will finally be subject to its forces: "Often Nature herself opposes us. What, then, can we do? She is irresistible" (281). A successful farmer is also a diligent student of nature. "If bountiful Nature is kind to us on the one hand, on the other she wills that we shall purchase her kindness not only with sweats and labour but with vigilance and care. These calamities remind us of our precarious situation" (297).

The enactment of the eighteenth-century agrarian ideal envisioned by Jefferson and Crèvecoeur and the expansion of farming into unsettled lands could be realized for little more than a century. As Emerson delivered his 1858 address to the Middlesex Cattle Society, land in the midregion of the United States was being purchased by private interests; and when Garland began writing his short stories two decades later, he was observing the real consequences of the rapid expansion into the western United States. The announcement by the United States government in 1890 regarding the closure of the American frontier was merely an official statement of what had been obvious to Garland and thousands of settlers who had been attempting to realize the agrarian dream in the earlier decade.[14]

The closure of the American frontier had more than an economic impact on aspiring farmers; it also resulted in psychological implications for the nation. The official loss of the frontier required that the American people confront and redefine their notion of democracy, which had hitherto been linked to an unlimited availability of land. This rethinking of an agrarian society also required a reconsideration of the role of the yeoman farmer, who depended on that land and who was the symbol of an egalitarian and virtuous society. Thus we see writers such as Smythe promoting new efforts at making the agrarian society possible—and others such as Garland lamenting its failure.

I consider here five writers whom few would address collectively. They are joined by their attention to agriculture and to the relationship among the agrarian experience, the human spirit, and human culture. Emerson, Garland, and Bailey consciously recognize farming as a means of realizing a deeper connection to nonhuman nature, while Norris and Smythe reveal the ways that farming increasingly disassociates from an awareness of terrestrial nature as it becomes entangled in human dramas. I open this study with a discussion of Emerson, who is known for considering the relationship between humans and nature, for attempting to elide perceptual boundaries that divided human consciousness from the larger cosmos of which we are a part. In his 1858 address "Farming," Emerson considers the relationship between the farmer and nature and provides us with several models for the ways that humans may conceive of and interact with the land. "Farming" is Emerson's attempt to apply his philosophy of nature to communal activities implicated in a social and economic complex. His views resonate with modern debates in environmental philosophy, which consider the relationship between perception and action. Emerson's work anticipates the conceptual tangle that emerges in the other four authors I examine, whose writings span the next seventy years.

Hamlin Garland and Liberty Hyde Bailey offer a view of agrarian nature that acknowledges the "nature" that surrounds and is implicit in agrarian lands. Both writers describe nonhuman nature as a physical reality and are attentive to the nuances and variations within it. Garland identifies farming as an activity that encompasses a physical and sometimes emotional relationship with nature. His deep attachment to the nonhuman nature of the Midwest has been overlooked by scholars who attempt to describe him within the literary categories of realism and naturalism—categories that focus on human society and culture to the neglect of nonhuman environments. In such works as *Main-Travelled Roads* (1891) and *Prairie Folks* (1892) Garland reveals that farming can be rewarding through its connection to nature, that it can be physically and spiritually degrading, and that it can be entangled in the larger economic structures of a society. What has been regarded as inconsistencies in Garland's literary vision may actually represent the difficult problems of describing the farming experience in all of its complexities.

My study of Norris centers in *The Octopus* (1900). Set in California's San Joaquin Valley, the novel is based on an uprising of farmers against the railroad in the late nineteenth century. The action is based in agriculture, but Norris employs farming primarily as an abstract vehicle for exploring larger philosophical questions surrounding nature and force. In considering how humans conceive of nature, he incidentally provides us with several models for how farmers may interact with and perceive the land. *The Octopus* reveals rhetorical inconsistencies similar to those I identify in Emerson's "Farming." Norris's epic reveals how a human activity such as farming is tangled simultaneously in a larger social and economic complex and in an amorphous nature. His literary act holds significant environmental implications. In developing his fiction, Norris abstracts the land, assigning it a symbolic function as the "scroll" on which he inscribes his epic of the wheat. In doing this, he ceases to represent the actual land and its various component entities, thereby eliding all that is not human or related to human activities.

Smythe shares Norris's tendency to abstract the land as he abstracts the Southwestern desert as a stage on which the American drama of reclamation will be played out. Smythe was an early booster of the reclamation movement in the American West. In *The Conquest of Arid America* (1905) he promotes the formation of communities organized around small, irrigated, family farms and casts his utopian scheme as a continuation of a drama of American progress—an act that has significant socioenvironmental implications for the way that the arid lands are ultimately transformed. Smythe's approach to agriculture embraces a mechanistic model of nature. For him the desert is a dehydrated Eden that will bloom and yield God's gifts when man ingeniously adds water. I explore Smythe's perceptions of the relationship between nature and American history and analyze his rhetoric to reveal how he facilitated a shift in public perceptions that resulted in the reclamation of the American West.

Like Garland, Bailey was raised on a farm. As an adult he followed the path of a scientist, becoming a horticulturist and an academic. Bailey called for the preservation and promotion of the small family farm and recommended the improvement of the conditions under which farmers labored; he also advocated the implementation of a public school curriculum that would teach rural children about the beauty of nature. Bailey's considerable body of writing reveals his concern both for the ways that farming damages the environments where it is practiced and for the way that farming might figure in a sound society. He argues for a consideration of the spiritual well-being of farmers, whose lives could be enriched through an appreciation of nature. Bailey believes in the doctrine of Christian stewardship of the land, but his vision of nature and agriculture is holistic. I consider how Bailey reconciles his scientific understanding with his spiritual experience of nature.

The writers I discuss here reflect a larger pattern characteristic ✓ of modern debates dealing with the relationship between humans and the environment. Emerson considers that we may regard the farm as an actual place where we manipulate nature or as a metaphoric space in which we explore our spirituality. Norris and Smythe carry this notion to a negative extreme and engage in literary acts that abstract the land into a symbolic entity on which the dramatic activities of humans are played out. Conversely Gar- ✓ land and Bailey, always aware of the effects of agrarian practice, reveal a richer understanding of the complicated relationship between nature, farming, and human culture.

Cultivating an

Uneven Land

L ATE IN 1858 Ralph Waldo Emerson delivered to the Middlesex Cattle Society an address that eventually came to be known
as "Farming." Although "Farming" is overlooked by most
scholars, it marks a chronological midpoint in Emerson's
career, written twenty-five years after his natural history essays
and twenty-four years before his death. Emerson's most important philosophical work was already behind him, and at this date
he was enjoying popularity on the strength of his earlier work.
"Farming" figures as a minor moment in Emerson's lengthy career, an event in a long series of lectures, addresses, and speeches
that typified his public life, but it also figures as a reflection of
Emerson's efforts to situate his philosophy of nature in a world
that was becoming increasingly complicated by modern technology. In "Farming," which was published in 1870 in *Society and
Solitude*, Emerson attempts to apply the abstractions of transcendental thought to a more practical realm. In doing so, he reveals
the difficulties inherent in adapting an individual spiritual practice to an activity such as farming, which in 1858 was increasingly
becoming entangled in a larger social complex.

"Farming" offers us a view of the farm as both the metaphysical
arena in which a transcendent relationship with nature might be

realized and a material entity on which the forces of human culture impinge. Throughout his career Emerson had examined human relationships with nature, but in his address to the Cattle Society, the tension between a metaphysical and a material interpretation of nature finds an expression that is illustrated in farming. The philosophical problems Emerson considers in "Farming" are hardly new; he introduced them in 1836 in *Nature*, when he developed his theory of nature, acknowledging it both as an abstract entity governing and reflecting human experience and as a material reality.[1] Emerson presumed that the material dimension of nature would be well-understood and self-evident, and he acknowledges this aspect of nature as "common nature," or "essences unchanged by man; space, the air, the river, the leaf" (*CW* 5). Emerson was primarily concerned, however, with exploring nature as an abstraction, an entity that might guide humans and lead them to transcendence; thus he focuses most attention on exploring nature in its more complex philosophical dimension:

> Philosophically considered, the universe is composed of Nature and the Soul. Strictly speaking, therefore, all that is separate from us, all which Philosophy distinguishes as the NOT ME, that is both nature and art, all other men and my own body, must be ranked under this name, NATURE. (*CW* 4–5)

Despite an attempt at defining his terms, Emerson nonetheless confounds his readers by slipping between these definitions throughout his discussions not only in *Nature* but in other works, such as "Farming." Emerson attempts to fix the definition of a term, *nature*, that has several meanings, but even his philosophical definition of the word suggests that nature may range from material substance to abstract essence.[2] This ambiguity opens his text to multiple interpretations, which become manifold when his discussion shifts from common nature to philosophical nature without apparent cues to the reader. Given this, *Nature* and his subsequent works that invoke the theories developed therein are laced with multiple layers of meaning, which are made only more dense when other definitions of the word *nature*, aside from Emerson's, are added to the semantic stew.[3] The semantic ambiguities inherent in any discussion of nature find full expression in "Farming."

To introduce Ralph Waldo Emerson into a discussion of nineteenth-century agriculture may seem peculiar. Emerson is most often recognized for his attention to transcendentalism and his concern for the condition of the human spirit rather than for matters such as agriculture, which center in material life. One need only look to the volumes published during Emerson's life to identify the relative unimportance of agriculture in his intellectual experience. The *Complete Works* includes only two pieces concerned specifically with agriculture: his 1858 address to the Middlesex Cattle Society and a short article published in the *Dial* titled "The Agriculture of Massachusetts." Most readers will concur that neither text is remarkable within Emerson's larger body of work.

Despite Emerson's apparent neglect of agriculture as a topic of intellectual scrutiny, it does figure into the context of his life—a context that pervades and permeates his journals, letters, essays, poetry, and addresses. This agrarian presence in his writing is understandable: the world into which he was born in 1803 was agrarian, and the New England of his day was populated by a people whose primary occupation was farming. The infant Emerson was born the same year that Jefferson completed the Louisiana Purchase, in an era when the yeoman farmer was still a reality in some regions and a possibility in others. Emerson's own father, William, was a minister, but like many, he supplemented his income by farming, both in Harvard, Massachusetts, and later in Boston, where he settled the family on several acres in a neighborhood dotted with orchards and pasture land (Allen 9). Decades later, in 1835, the adult Emerson moved permanently to nearby Concord to settle in a town sustained by an agrarian economy—an atmosphere that, he acknowledged, favored "the permanence of families" (Brooks 3). Although Emerson was by no means primarily a farmer, he nonetheless observed, and occasionally participated in, local agricultural fairs.[4] Like his neighbors, he took pride in his orchards and entered his fruit in competitions at the local agricultural shows. And like his father, he supplemented his income with the sale of produce raised on his land.[5]

The agricultural context of Emerson's life is apparent in his earliest work, where he employs farming as a metaphor for the practice of his larger philosophy. In "The Uses of Natural History," Emerson considers how students of natural history can enjoy the benefits of nature. By moving the locus of study outdoors, they will enjoy benefits from a contact with nature; such study will have a "salutary effect upon the mind and character" by teaching the student to discriminate among objects of the natural world, which can then be applied to one's self understanding (EL 1: 19). He suggests that those who enjoy the greatest opportunity for studying natural history are the "practical naturalists," people who routinely work out of doors: farmers, hunters, shepherds, and fishermen (6). Such people are in the position to come into "acquaintance with the properties of water, of wood, of stone, of light, of heat, and the natural history of many insects, birds and beasts" (6). He underscores that through an intimate experience of nature, individuals will benefit both their spiritual and their physical health. Emerson suggests that the farm is a legitimate arena for engaging with nature, and it may figure as the site for discovering the wonders of natural history.

In "The Uses of Natural History" Emerson develops farming metaphors to explain how the individual will learn about nature. Here Emerson creates two currents of meaning and speaks of farming both as a concrete activity that occurs within a material realm and as a conceptual activity that fosters spiritual illumination. He tells us that the individual who "cultivates" the study of natural history will enjoy its "salutary effect upon the mind and character" (19). He draws on Gilbert White to develop an extended metaphor in which the earthworm figures as an agricultural model: "Who are those that hoe and harrow the surface of the ground to keep it in a state of looseness fit for tillage, and to make the fallow land penetrable to the roots of the grasses and to the germination of forest trees? The Earthworms" (19). In borrowing from White, Emerson suggests that earthworms are "little gardeners and farmers" who, through their participation in a natural order, contribute to its organic whole. This use of a farming metaphor serves two rhetorical ends for Emerson: he illustrates how farming might figure as a metaphor for spiritual practice and as an activity in which his theories of nature might be applied. Emerson also introduces the distinctly democratic potential for the study of natural history, which was gaining increased popularity as an avocation. By directing his audience to the possibility that natural history and agriculture intersect, he argues that Americans, the majority of whom were engaged in some type of farming, have access to the spiritual and physical benefits of nature. By situating the study of natural history, however, in activities such as farming and mining, which also have an economic and political basis, Emerson ensures that the individual will be entangled in society.

Emerson's journals also reflect the way in which he was drawing on his experiences in agriculture to provide him with metaphors for his philosophical thoughts. Several of his 1838 entries consider the way that farming might figure in the formation of character and thus might enter into the transcendental experience. Emerson admires his neighbor, George Minott, as "a man of no extravagant expectations; of no hypocrisy; of no pretension. He would not have his corn eaten by worms,—he picks them out & kills them, he would have his corn grow, he weeds & hoes every hill; he would keep his cow well, & he feeds & waters her" (*JMN* 7: 12–13). Emerson appreciates the simplicity of Minott's life, which is defined by the natural features of the world he inhabits. Minott is a model of spiritual practice, embracing his farm as a dimension of nature, which, as Emerson had argued two years earlier, is a dimension of an overarching human spiritual nature. As a farmer of the spirit, Minott plucks the metaphorical worms that might impede his growth; he deals with such unpleasant yet expected annoyances as predatory plants and insects that could threaten his crop and his spiritual welfare. Minott tends his garden well that he might enjoy its fruit, which is also his physical sustenance.

Emerson interprets Minott as practicing a simple habit; he describes the farmer working alone, enjoying not just a material benefit but also a spiritual benefit from his activity.

Emerson himself also kept a garden, which he appreciated for the way it enabled him to meditate. As he writes in 1839,

> I know of no means of calming the fret & perturbation into which too much sitting[,] too much talking brings me so perfect as labor. I have no animal spirits[;] therefore when surprised by company & kept in a chair for many hours, my heart sinks, my brow is clouded, & I think I will run for Acton Woods, & live with the squirrels henceforward.
>
> But my garden is nearer, and my good hoe as it bites the ground revenges my wrongs & I have less lust to bite my enemies. I confess I work at first with a littel venom, lay to a little unnecessary strength. But by smoothing the rough hillocks, I smooth my temper; by extracting the long rootes of the piper grass, I draw out my own splinters; & in short time I can hear the Bobalink's song & see the blessed deluge of light & colour that rolls around me. (*JMN* 7: 211)

In these early years, farming figures for Emerson as both a source of solace and the locus of important lessons about the character of the physical world. In 1839 he considers the limitations of formal education and observes:

> We are shut up in schools & college recitation rooms for ten or fifteen years & come out at last with a bellyfull of words & do not know a thing. . . . We do not know an edible root in the woods. We cannot tell our course by the stars nor the hour of the day by the sun. . . . We are afraid of a horse, of a cow, of a dog, of a cat, of a spider.

Emerson praises fathers who would send their sons outside, into the woods and the farm, which he suggests is the right school:

The reason of my deep respect for the farmer is that he is a realist & not a dictionary. The farm is a piece of the world, the School house is not. The farm by training the physical rectifies & invigorates the metaphysical & moral nature. (*JMN* 7: 238)

The salutary effect of farming is available to the boys and men who would recognize its lessons.[6]

These early journal notations suggest Emerson recognizes the farm as a site for intellectual and spiritual inquiry, a place where one might discover what is most essential about life. The farm figures as an abstract essence—that is, an expression of nature— but it is also a material fact, a realm that figures in an actual economy. Emerson tells us that the farmer will not enjoy the material wealth that is increasingly shaping the perceptions of city folk. He suggests that "A Boston doll who comes out into the country & takes the hoe that he may have a good table & a showy parlor may easily be disappointed." Nonetheless, the diligent farmer will be in the position to discard the materialism of "living for show" and "take Ideas instead of Customs" and "see to it that 'the intellectual world meets Men everywhere' in his dwelling, in his mode of living" (*JMN* 7: 219). These ideas reflect those suggested in *Nature*: the purpose of nature, Emerson suggests, is to assist man to transcend matter. For the farmer, agrarian nature contains all the wisdom necessary to conduct oneself in a spiritually appropriate manner.[7]

While Emerson reflects openly on the idea of the farm in his journals, his references to farming are veiled and transposed in agricultural metaphors in his public works. Early in 1841 he introduced "the doctrine of the Farm" to a public audience.[8] He explains that "every man ought to stand in primary relations with the work of the world" and that the farm provides an appropriate venue for achieving this relation. He underscores that he offers the farm as merely a model for how one might engage in a spiritual practice with the world: "I do not wish to overstate this doctrine of labor, or insist that every man should be a farmer" (*CW* 152).[9]

Later that year, Emerson published his first series of essays, which included "Self Reliance" and "History." In "Self Reliance" he employs a farming metaphor to illustrate the necessity for developing one's talents: "There is a time in every man's education when he arrives at the conviction that . . . though the wide universe is full of good, no kernel of nourishing corn can come to him but through his toil bestowed on that plot of ground which is given to him to till" (EFS 29). "History" reflects a more complex exploration of the farming metaphor, which enters his discussion as he explores the tensions between nomadism and agriculture; the agrarian theme reemerges as he ponders how to balance motion with stasis. Agriculture represents a tendency for domestication, which for Emerson poses the risk of monotony. With nomadism, however, one runs the risk of dissipating physical energy; "intellectual nomadism" carries with it an even greater risk: it "bankrupts the mind" (EFS 17).

UNTIL 1858 Emerson had touched on agricultural themes in his private writing and had invoked agricultural metaphors in his public work that enhanced his discussions of other topics, but he had not focused his scrutiny on agriculture or attempted to situate it within his philosophical framework. In "Farming" Emerson brings his philosophy of nature to an agricultural milieu to consider how farmers may realize spiritual rewards through their work. Rather than attempt to fully characterize the relationship between the farmer and nature, Emerson presents seemingly contradictory views as he attempts to situate the farmer *within* nature. He suggests that farmers exist in a natural order to which they must adapt, that farmers are the minders of a factory created by God, and that farmers, through their knowledge of science, possess the tools with which they may dominate agrarian nature.

Emerson seems to be exploring several conceptual models of how humans may interact with their habitat—models that correspond to those with which modern environmentalists grapple: ecocentric egalitarianism, which identifies humans as a species inherently no more valuable than any other species within a complex natural network; what I call "mechanistic anthropocentrism," which identifies humans as separate from and superior to nature, which they dominate; and stewardship, which charges the farmer with a responsibility to care for nature, which will reward him. This shift from one conceptual model to another speaks to Emerson's efforts to situate human consciousness and spirituality within the amorphous realm of nature, which has both concrete and abstract dimensions.[10]

"Farming," which was originally conceived as a public speech, represents Emerson's attempt to apply his philosophy of nature, not just to individual practice but also to communal activities that involve a social and economic complex in which agriculture is practiced. The address figures as a synecdoche of Emerson's world, its circularity representing a rhetorical resistance to a monolithic view of the relationship between the farmer and nature. In his earlier work Emerson suggests that transcendence is achieved in solitary connection with nature, and in "Farming" he suggests that agriculture may provide opportunities for such an experience. He emphasizes throughout the address, however, that agriculture is implicated in the larger community and marketplace. Because farming is enmeshed with society, its potential to figure as a spiritual practice is always at risk, existing as it does between the often conflicting forces of unmediated nature and civilization.

In the opening paragraph of "Farming" Emerson reveals that he will be discussing nature in both its common and its philosophical definitions, and he acknowledges the ambiguity of these terms by speaking of "the earth" when referring to an unambiguously physical realm. The farmer, he suggests, exists "close to Nature" but "obtains from the earth the bread and the meat" (W 7: 137). This sentence introduces Emerson's discussion of the farm, which, like nature, has both common and philosophical definitions. The farm, in its common definition, might be defined as that realm wherein "essences unchanged by man" are in fact transformed. In its philosophical definition the farm is an expression of nature—which, as he suggested in *Nature*, may be the reflection of man, the medium through which the farmer might come to know and understand God and transcend material existence.[11] These several meanings accrete through the address as Emerson defines farming as an activity of spiritual utility to the farmer.

Emerson begins "Farming" by initially identifying the farm as a pastoral realm. Farmers, he says, are engaged in the "pleasing arts"; such individuals are innocent yet dignified creatures who bear the "manners of Nature" in a space that figures as a refuge from the urban scene:

> All men keep the farm in reserve as an asylum where, in case of mischance, to hide their poverty—or a solitude, if they do not succeed in society. . . . Poisoned by town life and town vices, the sufferer resolves: "Well, my children, whom I have injured, shall go back to the land, to be recruited and cured by that which should have been my nursery, and now shall be their hospital." (*W* 7: 137–38)

Emerson invokes a pastoral tradition when he suggests that human life enjoys a purification when its locus is shifted from the city to the country. The hints of pastoralism embedded in this early passage are completed near the end of "Farming" when Emerson asserts that "uncorrupted behavior" is found among those living in the presence of nature (153). Herein Emerson establishes the farm as a utopia—the kind of world that Michel Foucault has suggested is an "unreal" space, that "present[s] society itself in a perfected form" (24). This pastoral utopia provides an escape from the incursions of society and represents an ideal space, extracted from confounding social influences, that would have been accessible to most of Emerson's audience. Unlike traditional utopias, which represent social alternatives to a prevailing order, Emerson's pastoral realm exists as a space wherein the individual may escape the spiritually corrupting influences of the city and enjoy an idyllic experience that, for Emerson, is an intimate understanding of nature.[12]

Because the pastoral utopia is valuable only for the way it provides an ideal space for spiritual work, Emerson's "Farming" does not linger over a vision of the farmer as a pastoral swain; instead, it focuses on the farmer as a student of nature and suggests a view that, if considered ahistorically, might be regarded as ecocentric egalitarianism. Emerson's farmer adapts to natural conditions when he "bends to the order of the seasons." The farmer practices a habit of patience that helps to develop a reverence and respect for nature, and he responds to the larger natural world, understanding that "the earth shall feed and clothe him; and he must wait for his crop to grow." This adaptation means that the farmer is bound to the earth. He "clings to his land as the rocks do," a notion implying that the farmer is subject to natural forces (*W* 7: 139).

Emerson suggests what we now might regard as an ecocentric view that recognizes the individual farmer as a part of a natural network. Entangled in this vision is the notion that the farmer, working in response to nature, is a solitary figure engaged in a solitary activity. Emerson's farmer is the "first man," an idea that is a twist on Jefferson's more pluralistic view of farmers as the chosen people of God. Emerson draws on the biblical imagery traditionally associated with American agrarianism, which identifies farmers as the cultivators of a promised land, but Emerson places his farmer in an ancient garden when he identifies him as the first man, the one to whom all men look with respect.[13] When Jefferson suggests that farmers are the chosen people, he invokes the image of a community engaged in a divine enterprise; conversely, when Emerson invokes the Adamic model, he suggests that the farmer functions in a solitary role and that his activities are centered in a personal relationship with God into which larger issues of community do not figure.

This individualistic view of the relationship between humans and nature seems to be an adaptation of the theories Emerson develops in his earliest work. In "The Uses of Natural History" Emerson suggests that the farmer is in the position to realize a serenity that comes with an experience of nature: "Dig your garden, cross your cattle, graft your trees, feed your silkworms, set your hives—in the field is the perfection of the senses to be found, and quiet restoring Sleep" (EL 11). This experience, however, depends on the autonomy of the individual farmer; the quiet restoring sleep of the fields will likely be found only when the farmer works his land in solitude. Like Emerson himself, whose famous transcendental moment as a transparent eyeball occurred in solitude, the farmer will find his in solitary communion with agrarian nature.[14] Emerson's allusion to crossing cattle and grafting trees, however, speaks to the incursion of society on the farmer's activities. While the farmer may enjoy a certain spiritual benefit from his communions with nature, he is nonetheless working in a world that, even in 1833, was increasingly influenced by scientific approaches to farming, directed at improving yields. The farm practice to which Emerson alludes in "The Uses of Natural History" figures in not only a spiritual but also a material economy.

Twenty-five years later, in "Farming," Emerson again points to an inherent tension between nature and culture. He begins his address by suggesting that the farmer works in response and adapts to nature, but soon Emerson acknowledges that this model does not quite accurately address farming, which entails manipulating nature. Thus he shifts from a model of the farmer as a passive figure aligned with nature to one that posits the farmer in a mechanistic relationship with nature. Emerson moves from suggesting that the farmer "clings to his land" to the idea that nature is a great and perfectly timed machine, of which the farmer is the minder. The farmer's task is to understand the machine; his tools in achieving that understanding are the sciences. This machine, however, is nonetheless a part of a natural network. Emerson tells us that "Nature works on the method of *all for each and each for all*" (W 7: 143). The study of science reveals that nature operates in "great circles"; the farmer's understanding of this fact will enhance his agriculture. Although Emerson's farmer begins as a minder of nature's machine, through the study of science he can manage nature within its larger order:

the earth is a machine which yields almost gratuitous service to every application of the intellect. Every plant is a manufacturer of soil. In the stomach of the plant development begins. The tree can draw on the whole air, the whole earth, on all the rolling main. The plant is all suction-pipe,—imbibing from the ground by its root, from the air by its leaves, with all its might (144).

By shifting to a mechanistic model, Emerson readjusts his view that the farmer is at the mercy of nature to suggest that the farmer can study nature and thereby manage and manipulate it.

In developing a model of the farmer as both the passive object of nature and the minder of its mechanism, Emerson reveals how models for perceiving human relationships with nature might be caught between seemingly contradictory forces. The farmer, Emerson suggests, is "timed to Nature, and not to city watches." He is situated within an agricultural economic system that increasingly operates like a factory. The farmer, who is governed by the seasons, is nonetheless caught within an economy that operates like a machine and is dependent upon a mechanized conception of time.[15] In addressing the "city watches," Emerson obliquely speaks to the way industry has reduced the "great circles" of nature to ever-smaller increments. The farmer is necessarily controlled by nature's timing, but he is also increasingly the subject of the "city clocks" of market forces.

As Emerson advances through his address, he attempts to reshape the image of the farmer as a passive figure by reinvesting him with not only power over a mechanistic nature but also power over society. As if to acknowledge that the farmer does not exist in isolation and that his activities are not directed solely at attaining a spiritual connection to nature, Emerson observes that the farmer produces the food upon which a society sustains itself; thus "In the great household of Nature, the farmer stands at the door of the bread-room, and weighs to each his loaf" (140). The farmer, Emerson suggests, is the mediator between nature and society. In this position, however, the farmer manages or minds nature—a role that, ironically, seems to further remove the farmer from the nature that is so vital to his spiritual well-being by shifting his attention from his relationship with nature to his relationship with society.

Emerson suggests that the farmer benefits society while nonetheless exercising control in that relationship. In doing this, Emerson also invokes the model of stewardship. The farmer not only experiences nature in a way that benefits him individually; he also manipulates nature toward the good of his country by improving raw nature: "He who digs a well, constructs a stone fountain, plants a grove of trees by the roadside . . . makes the land so far lovely and desirable, makes a fortune which he cannot carry away with him, but which is useful to his country long afterwards" (141). In asserting that the farmer improves the land, Emerson modifies the model we might regard as ecocentric egalitarianism, which identifies the farmer as clinging to the earth, and he supplants it with one suggestive of stewardship, which situates the farmer as a servant of God and a protector of the land.[16] This model shifts the role of the farmer as merely one more element within an organic nature and places him within a hierarchy, dominating yet nonetheless protecting nature. As Paul B. Thompson has observed, stewardship, while emphasizing the protection of nature, is "conceived as a duty ethically subservient to production; hence, when stewardship would entail constraints on production, duties to nature seldom prevail over the productionist ethic" (72). While Emerson thus addresses his farmers on the issue of improvement and protection, suggesting that the farmer is "the continuous benefactor" of nature, he acknowledges that this beneficence is directed at increasing the value of the land.[17] This ethos is more compatible with capitalism. Emerson's readjustment of his model may represent a rhetorical response to anticipated objections to a model of an organic network that would not contain a mechanism to allow for one species to claim a larger share of nature's wealth than another. Moreover, stewardship offers a model of participation in the economic industrial system, which an organic network or ecocentric egalitarianism would not.

Emerson takes this notion still further, however, in speaking to his audience—among whom, no doubt, were abolitionists—and alludes to the extent to which the farmer is implicated in a larger political complex: the farmer not only brings a new "wealth" to the land; he subverts slavery. Emerson argues that a personal investment in the land that comes only through labor in the field will most effectively counter the forces of slavery. Farmers are not plantation owners; farmers work the land themselves rather than rely on the forced labor of slaves. Nature not only influences the individual farmer; it figures in the shaping of entire nations. Emerson suggests that as the farmer acquires an understanding of how nature works, he improves the land, which ultimately figures in the integrity of the larger social structure. When the farmer lays tiles and drains boggy fields, he exposes a rich soil: "These tiles are political economists, confuters of Malthus, and Ricardo; they are so many Young Americans announcing a better era—more bread" (150). Emerson responds to Malthusian predictions of overpopulation while simultaneously invoking America's mythic capacity to sustain an ever-growing population. Emerson looks to the West, where the farmer, using his great understanding of nature, will work in companion with the land.

Emerson concludes "Farming" by returning to the realm of nature and its powerful and positive influences on the farmer. His closing paragraph once again isolates the farmer within nature, where he is the passive and uncorrupted figure working under the control of its larger forces. The address concludes on a satisfying note, but only because Emerson has effectively returned us to the sphere of the individual who experiences a relationship with nature that is isolated from the larger complex of social influences.

As in many of his essays, in "Farming" Emerson does not follow a straight course that leads us through a set of logical arguments to a clear conclusion. He discusses the farm, the farmer, and the activity of farming and describes how these can operate simultaneously within actual and metaphoric realms. Roger Corrington argues that Emerson describes the farmer as a "living symbol of nature" (20). Indeed, Emerson implies this notion, but he also indicates that the farmer figures as more than a symbol: the farmer "stands close to Nature," a role that offers him access to the truths embodied therein, but the farmer must also know and manipulate a complex of natural conditions. Emerson shifts between depicting the farmer as adapting to nature ("He bends to the order of the seasons") and identifying the farmer as one who masters an aspect of nature, the earth: "The earth works for him; the earth is a machine which yields almost gratuitous service to every application of the intellect" (144).

When we consider the various views of nature with which Emerson works, agriculture occupies an ambiguous position. If nature is no more than that suggested in Emerson's definition of common nature, "essences unchanged by man," then the farm may well figure as an unnatural realm—a fact that may explain how Emerson seems to speak comfortably of the farm as a kind of machine and the farmer's relationship with it as mechanistic. Deep ecologists may argue that such a relationship necessarily results in an alienation from rather than an intimacy with nature. Indeed, one may argue that perceiving nature as a machine might encourage a form of farming that would be highly technical and mechanized. Gay Wilson Allen, observing that Emerson may not have been "uncompromisingly opposed to industrialism" (421), points to an entry in Emerson's journal in which he describes "picturesque traits" associated with the construction of the railroad in the Walden woods. This view finds further support by the way in which Emerson addresses technology and farming in his essay. It also points to the extent to which Emerson may have been caught in the rhetoric of capitalism—which, Carolyn Porter argues, distilled capitalism into industrialism, and industrialism into "technological sublime" (78–79). However, Emerson also suggests that farming may be "natural" and therefore could figure as an outward manifestation of an inward experience—that it could, in essence, represent one of the "signs of natural facts" on which farmers might draw in their own spiritual improvement.

This pervasive ambiguity about where farming fits in Emerson's picture points to the problem of working with models for perceiving human relationships with nature and the related difficulty of classifying certain human activities such as farming as inherently ecocentric or anthropocentric. In "Farming" Emerson tells his audience that "The lesson one learns in fishing, yachting, hunting or planting is the manners of Nature" (W 7: 139) a statement suggesting that an important aspect of farming is the understanding of nature it offers. This message loses its potency, however, to more pressing social concerns. As much as Emerson may attempt to focus in "Farming" on the activity of the individual, he nonetheless repeatedly slips into a discussion that embraces and reflects society.

Emerson shifts among various models to explain the relationship between the farmer and nature. He establishes a hierarchy that positions nature at its apex, governing the farmer. The farmer is the confidante of nature: "He has grave trusts confided to him." But he also mediates between nature and society: "It is for him to say whether men shall marry or not" (140). Emerson suggests that through their relationship and knowledge of nature, farmers are privileged. In fact, however, New England farmers of 1858 were experiencing an ever-dwindling influence as the manager of the nation's bread-room. By the mid–nineteenth century, large-scale Midwestern farms had essentially forced New England farmers to become highly specialized in their production of perishable items that could be sold locally. Grain was shipped by way of canals and railroads from western farms to eastern markets.[18] New England farmers were competing with the more technical factory farms of Midwestern states, whose products could be sold more cheaply than similar locally produced goods (Cochrane 74); thus farmers who had been slow to adopt newer farm methods and equipment began to introduce newer technologies into their agricultural practice.[19] Although they had traditionally resisted scientific approaches to agriculture, New England farmers began to adopt the practices of western farmers, which were more efficient and which, coincidentally, relied on machinery that removed the farmer from his intimate association with the soil and plants that comprised the realm Emerson regarded as central to the transcendent experience.

Within this context Emerson could not credibly promote his

idealized view of the farmer as existing only as the handmaiden of nature. Thus during the course of his address, he gradually modifies that model to suggest that the farmer, through his intimate understanding of nature, figures as the minder of the agrarian machine. This concept still promotes the view that the farmer is more than a solitary figure bending to nature. Emerson, suggesting that the earth is a great factory, points to the ways that the farm is a natural version of New England industry. The farmer is the manager of a machine of colossal proportions: "The diameter of the water-wheel, the arms of the levers, the power of the battery, are out of all mechanic measure; and it takes him long to understand its parts and its working" (142). This understanding will continue to benefit the farmer; his life is made richer by knowing nature, which imparts spiritual rewards, but the relationship between the farmer and nature is strained under the mechanistic images that drag the individual ever-further from "essences unchanged by man" into the realm of New England factories.[20]

In addressing the notion of the farm, Emerson struggles to contain it within the realm of nature, but ultimately he cannot extract it from the influences of civilization. The farmer, he suggests, is a "hoarded capital of health, as the farm is the capital of wealth" (140). As the capital of health, the farmer is a part of a spiritual economy in which his habit of mind and his labor yield spiritual rewards. But perhaps more important to Emerson's *audience* is that the New England farm represents a capital of wealth. In drawing this parallel, Emerson collapses his effort to excise farming from society. He faces an audience who, in the preceding twenty years, had seen their practice of farming transformed.

In "Farming" Emerson simplifies the concept of the farm by directing his focus from larger communities of people to solitary figures. This move, which has a historical dimension, effectively reduces the farm to the ground where the individual interacts with nature rather than an entity entangled in the larger culture. Emerson was familiar with the farm as an instrument of social reform, particularly through his peripheral association with the utopian experimental community Brook Farm. Through his friendships with George Ripley, Bronson Alcott, Margaret Fuller, and others, Emerson briefly considered participating in the commune. In 1841 Ripley had hoped to persuade Emerson to invest in the farm and join in his experiment in communal living, but he was finally unsuccessful. Emerson suggests in his journal that his joining Ripley would have violated his own belief in the ways in which social change is accomplished: "to join this body would be to reverse all my long trumpeted theory, and the instruct which spoke from it, that one man is a counterpoise to a city,—that a man is stronger than a city, that his solitude is more prevalent & beneficent than the concert of crowds" (*JMN* 7: 408). Allen observes that Emerson was reluctant to become entangled with the commune despite Ripley's arguments about the merits of farming as a means to attain a natural union between intellectual and physical labor (364). In a letter to Ripley he admitted, "I am very discontented with many of my present ways & bent on mending them; but not as favorably disposed to his Community of 10 or 12 families as to a more private reform" (cited in Allen 364). Emerson resists an involvement with Brook Farm as a vehicle of reform politics; the issue of a connection to nature apparently does not figure in his decision.

In his 1844 address, "The Young American," Emerson alludes to Brook Farm and condemns such communal efforts at social reform for the way that they emphasize the social to the neglect of the spiritual:

> These communists preferred the agricultural life as the most favorable condition for human culture, but they thought that the farm, as we manage it, did not satisfy the right ambition of man. The farmer, after sacrificing pleasure, taste, freedom, thought, love, to his work, turns out often a bankrupt, like the merchant. . . . Here are the Etzlers and mechanical projectors, who with the Fourierists, undoubtingly affirm that the smallest union would make every man rich;—and, on the other side, a multitude of poor men and women seeking work, and who

cannot find enough to pay their board. The science is confident, and surely the poverty is real. If any means could be found to bring these two together! (W 1: 381–82)

The farmer of a commune, Emerson suggests, is investing in a material economy. The life of the traditional farmer is not suited to the social goals of the farm communists because his actual cultivation figures, in contrast, in a spiritual economy. In communes such as Brook Farm, the needs of the individual are subordinated to the needs of the community.

Emerson speaks literally to the diminishing economic returns of the New England farmer who practices farming according to methods that are not competitive with the increasingly commercial farm markets. In doing so, Emerson simultaneously identifies the fissure that forms when the spiritual dimension of farming is placed in opposition to the material, economic dimension. Recognizing that the solitary farmer cannot sustain his enterprise, Emerson laments the intrusion of commerce into farming, alluding to the farm associations that "fix the price of bread, and drive single farmers into association in self-defence; as the great commercial and manufacturing companies had already done" (382–83). The associations, for Emerson, represent a collective force analogous to industrial monopolies. In working collectively, they enjoy a market position with which an individual farmer cannot compete. These bodies, however, are more significant for the way they represent an opposition to the individual who somehow combines farming with the cultivation of the spirit. Emerson seems to conflate such endeavors as Brook Farm with farm collectives, which were formed as commercial bodies to gain bargaining strength in a market economy. As organized social bodies, however, the farm communes, the farm collectives, and industry resemble the "patriarchal form of government [that] readily becomes despotic" (375). The individual farmer suffers, and the solitary individual is elided almost entirely.

Emerson's resistance to collective social transformation undergoes little revision and is transposed in "Farming" into an oblique reference to abolition when he suggests that "The man that works at home helps society at large with somewhat more of certainty than he who devotes himself to charities." Slavery is best defeated, he argues, by the farmer who "stands all day in the field, investing his labor in the land, and making a product with which no forced labor can compete" (*W* 7: 141). In speaking to his audience of farmers, Emerson adapts his model of individualism to agriculture and defies a popular image of the farmer as a part of a larger community that forms the foundation of democratic society. His view is not incompatible with a Jeffersonian model of the farmer; rather it is highly idealized, extracted from the actual context of the nineteenth-century world.

In "Farming" Emerson repeatedly steps into the realm of politics and then withdraws. When he asks, "Who are the farmer's servants?" he opens himself to consideration of slavery. He answers his own question, however, by suggesting that they are "Not the Irish, nor the coolies, but Geology and Chemistry" (142).[21] This statement rhetorically shifts Emerson's discussion from the realm of the political and redirects it to the realm of science—an especially significant alteration, given the era in which he presents "Farming." His 1858 audience of New Englanders were affected by slavery, the fugitive-slave law, the shortage of labor, and the possibility of increasingly technological farm practices. This redirection of a potentially contentious topic has a rather cryptic dimension because Emerson shifts from the actual world of farm labor to the abstract world of geology and chemistry. This move may be interpreted as redirecting our attention away from the insubstantial concerns of society to the more important spiritual concerns of nature.

Emerson spoke to an audience who was likely all male, and his address assumes that the farmer will also be male. The relationship between the farm and domestic life must also be considered, for Emerson presents a view of the farm and farmer that extracts him not only from society but also from the personal relationships of family that were deeply intertwined with farm life. Just as the farm figures as the ground where nature and civilization meet, it figures as the ground where family and society meet. In his essay "History" Emerson explores the concept of history and its value to men and suggests that the influences of family and society converge in the farm. Of significance here is Emerson's suggestion that history functions as a vehicle for examining human relationships with nature. History is the record of the universal mind embodied in every man. Farming enters Emerson's discussion as he considers the tensions between nomadism and agriculture; the theme reemerges when he considers how one might balance motion with stasis. Emerson associates agriculture with domestication, which carries the risk of monotony. Conversely, nomadism introduces the risk of dissipating physical energy. Intellectual nomadism poses an even greater risk, which is bankruptcy of the mind. Emerson argues for a careful balance between nomadism and domesticity and advises that one never stray too far from a domestic ground where ideas can be considered without excessive distraction; conversely, one must work against the dullness of both body and mind that comes with stasis.[22]

This tension between nomadism and domestication—which might be translated into one between the masculine and the feminine—Emerson codes in "Farming" as a relationship between the masculine farmer and feminine nature. He opens "Farming" by erasing female presence and claiming for the farmer acts that are usually regarded as feminine: "The glory of the farmer is that, in the division of labors, it is his part to create" (W 7: 137). Feminine labor is elided from the agrarian scene, and the task of creation belongs exclusively to the masculine farmer. Emerson then goes on to decipher the actions of the farmer, which are always in response to a feminine nature. The farmer claims within the society the traditional role of the housewife as he "stands at the door of the bread-room." The farm is the realm of the male farmer; his household operates under the rule of a feminine nature—which, Emerson also suggests, might be dominated through an acute understanding of its mechanism. This feminine nature manifests in the elements that the farmer manipulates and that ultimately will "grow in plants and animals and obey the thought of man"

(144). Under his rule, feminine nature "turns her capital day by day" (145) and enables the farmer to participate in the larger economy.

Although Emerson acknowledges the role of feminine nature in the farmer's enterprise, he ignores the contributions made by real women to the farm capital; instead, the farmer stands as a solitary figure, solely responsible for the successful management of the farm. Emerson alludes to family members—who no doubt do contribute to the farm's success—only once, when he invokes the notion of American progress: "As his family thrive, and other planters come up around him . . . the new generation are strong enough to open the lowlands" (152). While the farmer enjoys a personal reward through his experience with a feminine nature, the actual farmer's wife is absent from the scenario. The farmer alone is responsible for the growth of the nation, which he accomplishes through his careful management and thoughtful sensitivity toward feminine nature.

✓ "Farming" is a philosophical Gordian knot that invokes multiple possible views for relating to the physical realm. Emerson draws on popular notions of nature as feminine while simultaneously participating in the elision of women from the agrarian economy. Both actual women and female nature are a part of the tools upon which the farmer draws in achieving his successful management of the earth. Because the farmer operates as an individual rather than as a member of a community, he figures at the apex of his own particular microagrarian hierarchy. He may be at the mercy of feminine nature, but through his ingenuity he also learns her ways and thereby comes to manage her. Similarly, as the manager of his farm, he subsumes under his aegis the contribu-
✓ tions of those whom he manages. Emerson adopts here an idyllic model of the farmer that parallels the image of Thoreau at Walden Pond, who planted a small plot of land and worked it alone.

Emerson's exploration of the various conceptual models to characterize the relationship between the farmer and nature suggests the problems inherent in describing relationships with nature in general terms. Emerson's tendency to depict farming as an activity that belongs only to the masculine experience is typical of most depictions of farming; it is a characteristic that will be evident in my succeeding chapters.

EMERSON IS sometimes faulted for promoting an anthropocentric ✓ worldview by identifying nature as a commodity for use in human spiritual development.[23] The environmental philosophers and historians critical of Emerson have argued for a worldview that places humans within a network of nature rather than at the apex of a hierarchy where a commodified nature might be exploited for human benefit. Their call for an ecocentric worldview represents an effort to shift human perceptions about the relationship between humans and their habitats from human needs exclusively to a view, or conceptual model, that identifies humans as figuring within larger biologic communities. In identifying how a worldview that originates from the position of human need has resulted in environmental degradation, many environmentalists—notably, deep ecologists—have argued not simply for a change in human behavior but also for a change in the perceptions and beliefs that shape their behavior. Many would argue that some belief systems, such as Christianity, promote an anthropocentric worldview, which ultimately sanctions behaviors that are environmentally deleterious, while other belief systems, such as Native American spiritualism, encourage a reverent attitude toward nature, a philosophy that promotes environmentally sympathetic behavior.[24]

Emerson might be approached as an object lesson to modern ✓ environmentalists who have explored various models for conceiving the relationship between humans and the world they inhabit. Many of the models they posit speak to the environmental effects of modern industrialism and emerge from an effort to identify the philosophical roots of negative environmental practices. One such conceptual model is anthropocentrism, which is faulted as a view that has assigned less value to nonhuman life than to human life. This view is frequently linked to mechanistic interpretations of nature that identify nature as operating according to laws that can be identified and understood. Some environmental philosophers have implicated mechanistic interpretations of nature in its "de-sacralization." Ecofeminists, in looking to the relationship between a female-gendered nature and its exploitation, have argued that as modern science demystified nature, its systematic domination followed.[25] Generally, environmental philosophers have argued that a mechanized view of nature has supported the development of modern industry, which has exacted a devastating toll on the environment.

Much of the criticism directed at Emerson results from an ahistorical evaluation of his ideas by critics who employ conceptual models developed in response to twentieth-century environmental problems to assess nineteenth-century thought. One cannot argue that Emerson does not posit nature as a commodity; he devotes an entire chapter of *Nature* to that theme. The careful reader, however, must acknowledge that Emerson's notion of commodity figured in a much larger effort to make sense of the ways that humans engage with nature. Trained as a minister, Emerson was concerned with human spirituality. In the early nineteenth century, when the understanding of the impact of human behavior on nature was nascent, Emerson drew attention to the possibility of perceiving the relationship between humans and nature in a new way. Just as modern environmentalists consider the ways that human perceptions of nature shape environmental practices, Emerson considered how perceptions of nature shape the spiritual and intellectual condition.

Environmentalists have argued that the resolution of environmental problems will likely depend on our developing solutions that acknowledge the dynamic interactions among the individual, society, and the environment. Although Ralph Waldo Emerson was unconcerned with the state of the environment per se, his work nonetheless focuses on the relationships among these three entities. "Farming" well demonstrates how interactions between humans and nature cannot be isolated from their social context. Emerson invokes a mechanistic model of nature to explain the work of the farmer, yet he simultaneously acknowledges the limitation of that model by suggesting the extent to which the farmer is subject to nature. That Emerson invokes such a model, however, makes sense when we consider that he was responding to social forces impinging on the farmer. The farmer always exists at the nexus of nature and culture, and in nineteenth-century New England, that culture was increasingly mechanized. Emerson shifts between mechanistic interpretations of nature and a larger organic model as he attempts to identify how the farmer may perceive his place both within nature and within a larger social order.

As Emerson wrote his address in 1858, he anticipated larger changes that were to come—changes that would transform the way agriculture would be practiced in the United States and the way agriculture would figure in America's notions about itself. The tensions he invokes will become increasingly evident through ✓ the nineteenth and early twentieth centuries as farming becomes technology- and science-based. "Farming" reflects the way future writers will struggle to position agriculture in relationship both with nonhuman nature and within the realm of human culture. Emerson situates the farm in a conceptual space that is wholly belonging in neither nature nor culture. He considers not only the way that agriculture is considered within an imaginative realm but also the way that conceptions of agricultural practice influence the environmental milieu in which it occurs.

Nature and the

Midwestern Farm

HAMLIN GARLAND was born in 1860, two years after Emerson presented his address to the Middlesex Cattle Society. These authors are united in this book through the shared context of agriculture. Although Garland, like Emerson, was born to agrarian life and to a world that embraced Jeffersonian values, their lives were quite dissimilar. Emerson was reared among the intellectual elite of New England, while Hamlin Garland began his life among the rustic farm folk of Wisconsin, Minnesota, Iowa, and later, the Dakotas. His education commenced in his early boyhood when he explored the rich biological realm that lay on every side of his various childhood homes. This realm, which he would later call "unadorned" nature, was defined by farm fields, woods, and prairies. Garland's early experiences of unadorned nature would appear in his writing, revealing his sensitivity to the plant and animal communities comprising the nonhuman environment surrounding the farm. Unlike Emerson, who appreciated farming as a conduit to nature and therefore to a greater self and to God, Garland never carried his thoughts to such an abstract plane. He understood nonhuman nature primarily as a terrestrial reality. Yet despite his relative philosophical simplicity, Garland, like Emerson, recognized an intangible value associated with agrarian nature, which was compromised by the influence of larger human cultural forces that were driving agriculture.

Garland began his formal education, if it might be described as such, in 1876 at a seminary in Osage, Iowa, a school from which he graduated five years later at age twenty-one. Even at that age, Garland craved a more sophisticated intellectual realm than could be found in the Midwest schools where he would teach; thus in 1884 he moved to Boston, where he hoped to undertake a course of study under the direction of the great minds at Cambridge. He soon discovered, however, that study at Harvard was an impossibility.[1] Undaunted, Garland undertook a course of self-directed study that carried him into urban libraries and public lecture and concert halls. His diligent pursuit of urban culture and scholarly connections eventually earned him teaching opportunities at a small private school. Soon a public lecture series began to earn Garland a regular audience for his scholarly work.

In 1887 Garland returned to the Midwest, where he rediscovered his own deep connection to the rural land he had left behind when he migrated east. His urban experiences had altered his √ vision; he returned to his boyhood home and its culture with a new perspective and a heightened awareness of the mean and difficult lives of the local people. His stories in *Main-Travelled Roads*, which were inspired by that visit, speak to the hardships of farming, but they also reflect his heartfelt affection for the land itself. In *A Son of the Middle Border* (1917) Garland describes his return to Osage, Iowa, and explains how that experience inspired the birth of his career as a fiction writer. He reveals retrospectively his reconnection to the land as he recounts his observations of the region beyond Chicago:

> Each weedy field, each wire fence, the flat stretches of grass, the leaning Lombardy trees,—everything was significant rather than beautiful, familiar rather than picturesque.
>
> Something deep and resonant vibrated within my brain as I looked out upon this monotonous commonplace landscape. I realized for the first time that the east had surfeited me with

picturesqueness. It appeared that I had been living for six years amidst painted, neatly arranged pasteboard scenery. Now suddenly I dropped to the level of nature unadorned, down to the ugly unkempt lanes I knew so well, back to the pungent realities of the streamless plain. (355)

For Garland, homecoming allowed him to tap into the basic elements of the land and to shed Eastern aesthetic standards and their related definitions of landscape beauty. He identifies what for him is most "real" about the land, which is a blending of nonhuman and human nature. His reengagement with his home region reflects an acceptance of the humble beauty of the land that is neither sublime nor grandiose. In recollecting this return, Garland does lapse into moments that suggest a familiarity with the concept of idealized sublime landscapes as he observes some settings through a veil of romantic prose: he considers an island on the Mississippi for its "noble trees" and imagines the "redman's canoe, the explorer's batteau, the hunter's lodge, the emigrant's cabin" (356) as historical elements of the land.

Garland also reconciles his love for the land with his observations of human life, commenting, "I had studied the land, musing upon its distinctive qualities, and while I acknowledge the natural beauty of it, I revolted from the gracelessness of its human habitations" (356). He reveals here that he perceives the land in two dimensions. One is centered in the native, nonhuman, biological elements of a setting; the other relates to human presence and the way that human interventions have resulted in disfigurement of landscape. Garland's interest in the way that humans influence a scene later finds its way into his short fiction dealing with agrarian life, which has generally been the focus of literary scholars, who regard them as evidence of Garland's realism. Seldom considered, however, is the way that Garland reveals a visceral affinity for the land itself, which possesses for him not only an aesthetic appeal but also certain ineffable "distinctive qualities." These qualities are embedded in the nonhuman nature of the place, in the topography, the geology, the plants, and the animals of the region. These elements of place claim a revered position in his cosmos and become even more profound when considered within the context and circumstance of human experience. Garland draws on his particular affinity for that land and addresses the relationship between the land and the humans who inhabit and farm that region.[2]

This deep connection to a region and its unique physical qualities is articulated as a theory of literature in Garland's single contribution to literary criticism, *Crumbling Idols* (1894). In the first essay in the collection, Garland argues for "the beginning of an indigenous literature" (7) that critics might respect rather than dismiss as merely provincial.[3] Garland unfolds his argument for a literature that illustrates the distinctive natural and cultural characteristics of a place. He defends his scholarly authority by acknowledging European writers such as William Wordsworth, Henrik Ibsen, Leo Tolstoy, and Alfred Tennyson, and he turns to the texts of the literary theorists of his age—Hippolyte Taine, Hutcheson M. Posnett, and William Dean Howells—to establish a substantial intellectual foundation for his own theory. By challenging the conservative critics of his day who disparaged American writers while encouraging an imitation of European literature, Garland implicitly justifies his own literary subjects: the humble people and the lands of the Midwest, where he had been raised.[4]

In *Crumbling Idols* Garland's theory of literature emphasizes a connection to place and thereby delineates his standard for good art. In "Local Color in Art" he suggests that the essence of local color resides in the rendering of the unique aspects of *human* culture in literature. Garland quickly shifts his focus, however, and makes the land itself the basis of local color. He tells us that local color writers "are rooted in the soil. They stand among the cornfields and they dig in the peat-bogs" (50). William Cullen Bryant and James Fenimore Cooper were influenced by "mighty forests and prairies" (51), and those same natural environments shaped the local color writers and their literature. In juxtaposing cornfields with mighty forests, Garland suggests that cultivated nature is as worthy a subject as sublime wild nature. In "New Fields" he tells us that "the artist must consciously stand alone before nature and before life" (23). A genuine literature speaks specifically to the place from which it emerges, and it reflects the differences among places: "It is the subtle differences which life presents in California and Oregon, for example, which will produce, and justify, a Pacific Coast literature" (21).

Despite his awareness of the significance of place, Garland is also a product of his literary environment, and he still regards not the land but the people as a primary focus of art. He suggests that in an ideal literature the land and nature form a backdrop, albeit a backdrop unique to a particular locale: "In this literature will be the shadow of mountain-islands, the sweep of dun plains, and the dark-blue mountain-ranges silhouetted against a burning yellow sky" (25–26). This literature, however, will reflect the unique features of place: "It will be such a literature as no other locality could produce, a literature that could not have been written in any other time, or among other surroundings" (26). Garland's theory of literature attempts to situate his deeply felt attraction for nature within the larger literary world that values the urban over the rural and places more importance on relationships between humans than those between humans and the nonhuman environment.

Garland falls into the same literary habit as Norris and Smythe in identifying the land as the backdrop to human drama, but he resists the impulse to abstract the land to the extent that they do. Torn between two literary habits, Garland writes stories in which the land acts as a stage for action while he simultaneously acknowledges that the land has a value independent of its utilitarian benefits. Even as he describes the nature surrounding and permeating the agrarian landscape in such stories as those in *Main-Travelled Roads*, Garland simultaneously focuses on human dramas to criticize the effect of farming on the lives of individual people. He is concerned with the physical hardship and cultural deprivation of the farm, and this concern dominates his work, even as he promotes a more subtle message about the beauty of the land itself.

At times Garland indulges exclusively in his affection for the land and the positive farm experience. In *Boy Life on the Prairie* (1899) he largely abandons his criticism of agrarian privation to indulge in a nostalgic retrospective of his boyhood farm life that exalts his experience of nature. The tension observed by Garland between the beauty of the land and the impoverished lives of its human inhabitants pervades his early stories. Yet many of his critics overlook this tension or read it as stylistic inconsistency.[5] Indeed, although *Main-Travelled Roads, Prairie Folks,* and *Other Main-Travelled Roads* are noteworthy for their realistic descriptions of agrarian life, one cannot fail to see Garland's obviously favorable, perhaps even idealized, view of the land.

Yet in shifting between realistic and romantic descriptions of the agrarian land, Garland dispels an idyllic vision of farm life as he simultaneously affirms it. This dual vision frequently creates a discontinuous quality to his work, though it also suggests his attempts at reconciling his personal experience of farming with a popular notion of agriculture as integral to America's beliefs about itself. He understands the negative as well as the positive dimensions of farm life. At times he seems to lodge an implicit attack on the agrarian ideal described by Jefferson and Crèvecoeur, to which many Americans of Garland's day adhered.[6] Through his realistic depiction of farm life, Garland exposes the actual rather than the idealized conditions of farming, thereby undermining the yeoman farmer as a positive symbol of the American every-man. Garland addresses two related notions: first, that farming exerts an ennobling influence over those who engage in it—an influence that is, in turn, reflected in the larger society; and second, that forces at work in the nineteenth-century economy are ultimately to blame for degrading farming as an occupation. These forces are embedded in the environment of human society and figure as the sometimes-attenuated expression of literary naturalism that appears in Garland's work.[7] He implies that farming might indeed become a more noble endeavor if market forces could be altered to favor the farmer. Ironically this assumption works to undermine his refutation of the agrarian vision.

GARLAND GENERALLY has received scholarly attention for his depiction of human conditions in his early work; his later work, which departs from social concerns, is often described as romantic and dismissed as trivial. I posit that throughout his career his works, while often lyrical, speak to a genuine affinity with the land, to the nonhuman nature of a scene. Unlike authors who distinguish between wilderness and the domesticated farmland, Garland asserts that the nature found on farms is worthy of acknowledgment. But Garland's literary community tended to neglect the value of describing nonhuman nature in literature. When writers detailed the unique characteristics of a region, they were praised for invoking local color, for their ability to describe the distinctive *human culture* of a place, such as that reflected in the work of Garland's peers Edward Eggleston and Mary Wilkins Freeman. Writers who considered nonhuman nature and had enjoyed popularity—such as Henry David Thoreau, Susan Fenimore Cooper, and John Burroughs—wrote about the natural beauty of uncultivated nature, and though popular, they were not afforded the respect of writers of "literature." John Muir, who was beginning to enjoy an audience for his writing, was especially appreciated for his descriptions of the grandiose landscapes of the Sierra Nevada, but few at that time would have classified him as a writer of great literary significance.

Garland had few immediate predecessors who described farmland as a valued natural landscape; moreover, among the literary establishment whose respect Garland craved, critical discussion of literature privileged a focus on human issues to the neglect of the nonhuman. Thus Garland carved out a new territory in American writing, one that shattered a romantic depiction of farming and offered a more realistic interpretation of the "nature" that had previously been depicted in these works. The tensions and sometimes contradictory messages inherent in Garland's early stories reflect his understanding that farming figures within the complex of human activities but yet is highly dependent upon an uncontrollable, nonhuman nature. What many literary scholars regard ✓ as textual inconsistencies—and as a failure to describe a unified vision—may actually represent Garland's attempt to acknowledge complexity. He suggests that many conditions can exist simultaneously in any given place or moment. His stories are populated with characters who are the victims both of an uncooperative nature (for instance, drought and pestilence) and of a larger economic system that places farmers at an economic disadvantage. These farmers, despite their hardships, derive a certain personal comfort from the natural beauty found in rural lands.

Garland's inconsistency resonates with the same rhetorical in- ✓ consistency that is apparent in Emerson's "Farming" and in Norris's *The Octopus*. None of these writers succeeds in reducing farming to an activity that can be described simply. Farming is highly connected to nature and yet entails the manipulation of nature. In its best moments, farming can be intensely spiritual through its relationship with nonhuman nature, but it also can be highly political with regard to its place in the larger society. Farming is subject to the unpredictable and sometimes troubling forces of nature even as its role in the nation's economy simultaneously subjects it to the forces of human culture. Garland seems to recognize this and attempts to encompass all of these realities of agriculture in his stories.

Scholars have attempted to describe Garland within the context of the literature of his contemporaries, variously classifying him as a realist, a naturalist, or simply a romantic idealist. Many look to what Garland called his "veritism"—that is, his harsh rendering of the details of farm life—as evidence of his realism. The range of critical efforts to define realism, however, speak to the imprecision of that category. George Becker acknowledges the difficulty of defining realistic literature but nonetheless describes it in terms of REALISM its major emphases: it takes as its subject that which is near at ↓ hand and available to observation; it tends to speak to experience in process, "dipping into the stream of life and is ideally all middle, without beginning or end" (29), and it suggests that humans are subject to deterministic forces. Becker regards realism as somewhat interchangeable with naturalism. Donald Pizer argues that realism is more diverse in its subject matter than Becker would suggest and that realism tends to embrace a subjective and an idealistic view of human nature (*Realism* 4). Warner Berthoff acknowledges that realism offers an unsentimental view of society at different levels, but he is more concerned with the impulse that drives the realistic movement in literature, which emerges with the rise of capitalism and industrialism (1–5).

Others look to Garland's depiction of farm families as the victims of the larger economic and social forces and argue that he is a naturalist. Lars Ahnebrink considers Garland, together with Stephen Crane and Frank Norris, as best expressing a naturalist philosophy "in technique and view of life" (60). Ahnebrink defines the naturalistic movement in American literature as a response to *social* problems of the late nineteenth century, such as the rise of corrupt corporate entities and the mean living conditions endured by immigrants, who were viewed through a lens influenced by the theories of modern science (1–20). Tracing the genesis of literary naturalism to nineteenth-century France and using Emile Zola as his model, Ahnebrink considers how naturalism adopted a pseudo-scientific method, relying on careful observation to render detail precisely. He considers the role of environment in naturalist fiction, suggesting that "The naturalist had learnt from Taine that the milieu was of primary importance in the life of the individual and as a result much of the space was given to description of setting" (24). The French naturalists tended to set their stories in industrial cities and slums—settings dominated by humans—and described their reality in brutal detail. They "extended the study of character to embrace the entire physical man with all his physical impulses and instincts and, in their emphasis on instincts and hidden, unconscious urges and the role these phenomenon play in human life, they contributed to a deeper understanding of man." Ahnebrink observes that naturalist writers stressed "the Darwinian concept of man and his affinity with organic nature and the influence of heredity and environment on the individual" (27–28).

The range of interpretations of literary naturalism is striking: Charles Walcutt traces naturalism to transcendentalism and its concern with intuition and scientific investigation; this transcendentalist stream splits in the late nineteenth century, one stream concerned with idealism and progressivism and the other with mechanistic determinism. Malcolm Cowley defines naturalism as "pessimistic determinism" and argues that the naturalist writers "believed that men and women were absolutely incapable of shaping their own destinies" (430). Pizer defines naturalism as containing tensions between commonplace subject matter and the heroic aspects of commonplace existence and between the deterministic qualities of life and an artistic resistance to determinism that affirms the value of human life.[8] More recently Lee Clark Mitchell has focused on the aesthetic dimension of naturalism and considered how it challenges the narrative assumptions of the readers who resist a determinist vision (xvii). June Howard considers naturalism as a literary genre rather than an ideology, while the new historicists, such as Mark Seltzer and Walter Benn Michaels, turn away from a focus on writers and characters and situate their critical discussions of naturalism within the larger context of the public discourse of its day.[9]

Implicit in all of these approaches to naturalism, and to the study of literature in general, is a focus on the influence of individual human behavior, human culture, and its institutions on human life. In discussions of literary naturalism, "nature" and "environment" are interpreted as dimensions of human culture. Nature is interpreted as the force that compels human behavior. This force may be embedded in biologically based inherited characteristics, which are deterministic. Conversely environment is interpreted as social milieu determined by economic class. Environment often encompasses setting but usually only when that setting is defined by human structures, such as a city. When literary lenses focus on the actual physical, nonhuman environment that appears in the texts of late nineteenth-century America, scholars tend to classify such texts as examples of realism or, more specifically, of local color. Such depictions of the nonhuman environment are acknowledged for the way they contribute to background and atmosphere rather than for the way they exert an influence on the characters. This scholarly orientation to the human elements of a text reflects a neglect of the role of extrahuman environment on humans or the influence of humans on the extrahuman environment. Ahnebrink suggests that the influence of environment figures prominently in naturalist fiction, but he and other scholars interpret environment as a milieu dominated and defined by humans rather than by such nonhuman features as topography, climate, or nonhuman biological elements. This interpretation reflects a larger tendency to ignore the actual and textual presence of nonhuman nature—a tendency that appears in most assessments by literary scholars, who focus on the political activism and messages of social reform that are embedded in Garland's early work.

In considering Garland as a literary figure, one might also consider the scholarly process employed in studying him, which entails a reading of texts for their figurative, representational dimension—an act that is certainly valid. Literary scholars, often approaching textual elements with an assumption that they necessarily represent metaphorical expressions of ideas, dismiss the notion that a text—in addition to presenting a figurative rendering of an idea—may also attempt to represent the thing in itself. For example, we may consider Melville's whale, Moby Dick, as a figurative expression of natural law, but we cannot overlook that Melville describes him as an actual whale. To some extent, Moby Dick is intended to represent a real whale inhabiting a real oceanic environment. However, when scholars consider Garland's stories, they tend to focus on the actions and behaviors of humans and regard the settings—primarily farms—as literary adjuncts to the larger metaphorical story. They look to the rendering of detail surrounding human elements, such as the farm structures and human culture, as a precise representation of actual conditions, but when and *if* they consider the nonhuman realms that permeate and surround those farms, they dismiss them as metaphorical elements intended by Garland to enhance his commentary on human issues. What occurs to humans in Garland's stories is considered only within the context of the social structures in which those humans participate, while what happens to those human characters within the context of the equally prevalent natural contexts is often overlooked. Thus most discussions of Garland, focusing on his efforts to address social injustice as it related to farming, overlook his messages about nonhuman nature.

Garland sought to differentiate himself from the naturalists. In *Crumbling Idols* he asserts that his model literature "will not deal with crime and abnormities" and instead will focus on "average types of character, infinitely varied, but always characteristic" (25). Like his peers, Garland is interpreting environment in terms of its human dimension, even as he acknowledges that nonhuman environment exerts a remarkable influence upon its human inhabitants. Curiously, naturalism examined the negative effect of environment: the most degraded human figure was one most influenced by environment; the highest was one who could transcend or overcome the malevolent influences that would result in criminal or pathological behavior; thus the highest expression of human behavior would be demonstrated in humans who revealed the ability to transcend environment. These theories were usually applied to human experience in urban settings; to some extent, Garland explored this force in his stories of *Main-Travelled Roads*. Generally, however, the negative effects of environment were linked most often to human-centered systems. The environment that we might think of as nonhuman nature exists parallel to human experience—always present, available, sometimes creating problems for humans but exercising a force over human lives that is inconsistent.

GARLAND'S EARLIEST stories—which he began to publish in 1887 and later collected in *Main-Travelled Roads* (1891), *Prairie Folks* (1892), and *Other Main-Travelled Roads* (1910)—emphasize Garland's displeasure with the nineteenth-century popular belief in an ideal agrarian society. This displeasure is evident in "Lucretia Burns," when Radbourn, the farmland radical, complains about the writers and orators who have "lied so long about 'the idyllic' in farm life, and said so much about the 'independent American farmer'" (*OMTR* 102). The average yeoman farmer of Garland's early stories suffers a mean existence, which is in marked contrast to the American vision of small farm life promulgated by Crèvecoeur and later embraced in nineteenth-century popular thought. Using realistic, hard-edged descriptions of the agrarian setting, Garland reveals the failure of the American agrarian dream, while also suggesting the spiritual possibilities that might be realized through a connection to the land.

With the goal of undermining the symbolic strength of the heroic American yeoman farmer, Garland exposes farm labor as degrading to the human spirit. His farmers are neither Jefferson's chosen people of God nor Emerson's bread-room managers: they occupy the lowest rung on a hierarchical economic and social ladder. Despite their labors, they seem to reap few rewards. His stories emphasize that the kind of labor required of the nineteenth-century farmer has profoundly destructive effects on both his physical and spiritual well-being. In "Lucretia Burns" Garland's school marm is deeply moved by the hardship suffered by the farm families whom she observes: "Men who toil terribly in filthy garments day after day and year after year cannot easily keep gentle; the frost and grime, the heat and cold, will soon or late enter into their souls. . . . If the farmer's wife is dulled and crazed by her routine, the farmer himself is degraded and brutalized" (*OMTR* 112–13). Garland hints at the way the land itself infiltrates the spiritual fiber of its inhabitants, but he emphasizes that physical toil transforms men into brutes and drains vitality from men and women alike.

Garland's stories describe how the hard labor associated with farming does not limit its influence to the adults who are actually engaged in it but afflicts the entire farm family. Revealing a deep sensitivity to the effects of poverty on human social conditions, he demonstrates the cycle of abuse that arises from impoverished circumstances. Parents who struggle with few rewards to produce the basic necessities of life have little energy to devote to their children. In "A Day's Pleasure" Mrs. Markham's exhaustion gives way to physical brutality. The children are described as animals, "chickens in new fallen snow" who snarl and snap like "cats and dogs" (*MTR* 174–75). Like those of the Markham family, the children of "Lucretia Burns" are compared to barnyard animals: they are "quarrelling at the well, and the sound of blows could be heard. Calves were querulously calling for their milk, and little turkeys, lost in the tangle of grass, were piping plaintively" (*OMTR* 81). Garland is unflinching in his depiction of conditions as he suggests that when parents are reduced to the condition of draft animals, their children are similarly reduced and become little more than livestock, requiring care and feeding so that they might be raised to a mature age when they can participate in the farm labor. In this suggestion that the children are little more than adjunct farm animals, Garland is also pointing to the ambiguous ✓ boundaries between human and nonhuman nature.

Garland underscores the physical, emotional, and spiritual deprivation of farm families in his depiction of the physical setting of farms and farm communities. In an effort to refute the image of the idyllic life to which Radbourn refers, Garland describes a Wisconsin farm village in "Up the Coulee" as a squalid burg, "unrelieved by a tree or a touch of beauty. An unpaved street, drab-colored, miserable, rotting wooden buildings" (*MTR* 55). Similarly the image of the idyllic farm is undone with our first view of the McLane farm, which is dominated by a muddy barnyard populated by cows "fighting the flies and waiting to be milked" (60). "Among the Corn Rows" introduces Julia Peterson pushing a plow through corn in the high heat of summer, "her face flushed with heat, her muscles aching with fatigue" (108). When Will comes to claim Agnes in "A Branch Road," he discovers her living in frank poverty, amidst broken furniture in dreary unpainted rooms that swarm with flies, while surviving on scant food of poor quality. Garland bludgeons his readers with the message that farm folk ✓ are degraded and brutalized not only by hard labor but also by their impoverished human-centered environment, void of physical beauty.

Garland's farm families, particularly the women, suffer miserable conditions, but Garland goes beyond simply illustrating those conditions to suggest that they result from social forces beyond the control of the farmers. These forces are rooted in the greed of a larger political and economic machine. Garland invokes a theme later claimed by Norris when he implies that American farmers have made their contribution to democracy and the agrarian society by performing their work in good faith but have been thwarted by a dwindling supply of cheap land and an economic system that benefits land speculators.[10] Instead of commencing their agrarian careers on inexpensive fertile land, nineteenth-century farmers must start out with the burden of expensive mortgages. His farmers complain that their hardship is linked directly to the high price of land—a condition that results from its dwindling availability. In "Among the Corn Rows" Rob laments that in Wisconsin, good land that could be profitably farmed was too expensive for the average man (102). In "Up the Coulee" a young farmer tells Howard McLane, "A few that came in early an' got land cheap, like McIlvaine, here—he got a lift that the rest of us can't get" (84). Only the early settlers could realize the hope of prosperity. The rest, as Howard's brother Grant suggests, are trapped in their situations: "a man can't get out of it during his lifetime, and I don't know that he'll have any chance in the next—the speculator'll be there ahead of us" (85). Even the Western territories, which once offered the promise of broad expanses of cheap land, are no longer a bargain: "Ten years ago Wes, here, could have got land in Dakota pretty easy, but now it's about all a feller's life's worth to try it" (85).

At the heart of the agrarian problem, suggests Garland, is the land speculator who arrives on the frontier before the farmer, buys high-quality farmland, and then sells it to farmers at a premium price. In "Under the Lion's Paw" he depicts the rapacious land speculators and their role in undermining the agrarian ideal. Haskins is a poor, honest, and none-too-smart farmer who has been reduced to destitution by pestilence that destroyed his Indiana farm. He rents a rundown farm from Jim Butler, a man who "believed in land speculation as the surest way of getting rich"

(146). In good faith Haskins and his family toil on the land and invest their money in the improvement of the farm with the intention of buying it from Butler at the end of their three-year lease. When the time comes, however, Butler has raised his asking price for the farm, explaining, "The land is doubled in value, it don't matter how; it don't enter into the question; an' now you can pay me five hundred dollars a year rent, or take it on your own terms at fifty-five hundred, or—git out" (154). That Butler's actions are supported by the law further enforces the tragic dimension to the tale.

A similar scenario is played out in *Jason Edwards* when Edwards moves west to escape the impoverished environment of the Boston tenements, only to face a greater impoverishment on the drought-plagued prairie. As in "Under the Lion's Paw" Garland suggests that Edward's failure is to be blamed on the speculator from whom he bought his land and who held his mortgage. Judge Balser, the villain of this tale, responds with indifference to the possibility that farmers will face bankruptcy after a third season of "short crops": "As I told Edwards when he first came . . . you can take your choice, go thirty miles from a railroad and get government land, or give me ten dollars an acre for my land. It was his own choice" (103). Garland invokes the naturalist ethic that runs through *The Octopus*, but unlike Norris, he suggests that predatory business practices are not merely part of a larger natural and amorphous force but lie within the sphere of human influence.

The idea that farmers might be saved from the malevolent influence of the speculator is implicit throughout Garland's stories and provides a balance to his vision of hopelessness. The agrarian dream could be realized, Garland suggests, if the economic advantage held by land speculators could be shifted to give the farmers an equal opportunity. Through the voice of Radbourn in "Lucretia Burns," Garland offers his reform plan that would establish that balance: "He outlined his plan of action: the abolition of all indirect taxes, the State control of all privileges that private ownership of which interfered with the equal rights of all. He would utterly destroy speculative holdings of the earth" (*OMTR* 104–05).[11] This proposal reflects Garland's personal belief in a system of single taxation that would not penalize the small farmer whose taxes increase as the result of improvements. It also reflects Garland's philosophy surrounding land use. Pizer has described Garland's beliefs in economic reforms through taxation, which would result in equalizing opportunity for all land owners. He suggests of Garland that "as a single-tax social reformer, he was not placing obstacles in the path of natural law; he was rather clearing the path of a man-made obstacle which was hindering the normal operation of natural law" (39). That obstacle is the land speculator who, according to Garland, holds an unfair advantage over the small farmer.

Garland often suggests that the land speculator is the primary cause of agrarian hardship, but he complicates that position when he acknowledges that farm failure may also result from the influence of nonhuman nature itself. In *A Little Norsk* the event that generates the action of the story is a blizzard in which Flaxen's parents are killed. The Dakota prairie is an unwelcoming, forbidding land: "The plain was almost as lone and level as a polar ocean, where death and silence reign undisputedly" (3). Brian Lee looks to "Under the Lion's Paw" and focuses on Garland's depiction of the plague of grasshoppers that drives Haskins to tenancy. Lee suggests that the pestilence that drives out Haskins "gives the story its naturalistic depth." The description of the grasshoppers that "wiped out" Haskins provides "a grotesque prologue and parallel to the rapaciousness of Haskin's new landlord" (62). This interpretation suggests that the plague of grasshoppers and the destruction of the crop figure as little more than literary devices that function as textual elements to illuminate our understanding of Butler, the villain of the story. One might consider, however, that Garland is also revealing that the life of Haskins is shaped as much by the forces of nonhuman nature—the grasshoppers—as by those of human nature, represented in Butler. In such a stance, Garland is demonstrating that in its shaping of human life, environment entails not only the influences of human culture but also those of nature.

In *Jason Edwards* the land itself poses an obstacle. Garland sets the action surrounding the farming venture in Boomtown, presumably in the Dakotas, in the late 1880s during a spell of protracted drought—the same drought that inspired Smythe to take up the cause of reclamation. The land on which the Edwards have chosen to farm is dry, almost barren:

> it was frightful on the prairie, bare of trees as a desert. The eyes found no place to rest from the hot brazen glare. . . . There was absolutely no fresh green thing to be seen, no cool glint of water, no pleasant shade—only a radiant, mocking, sinister sky. . . . The farmers toiled at their scanty crops of hay, and eyed the sky with prayers and curses alternating on their lips. Every year at this same date those blighting winds had blown. (132)

Because they have no other options for survival, the farmers stubbornly try to farm a land that steadfastly resists their efforts. Although the farm was to offer a new start and an escape from tenement living, it ultimately proves to be harsher than the urban realm. Garland acknowledges that the farmer is as much at the mercy of nature as of culture. When following the storm that destroys the Edward's crop, the journalist, Reeves, ponders the scene of the disaster: "Reeves felt again the force of Nature's forgetfulness of man. She neither loves nor hates. Her storms have no regard for life. Her smiling calms do not recognize death. Sometimes her storms coincide with death, sometimes her calms run parallel to men's desires. She knows not, and cares nothing [*sic*]" (182).

Garland invokes a theme that Norris will reiterate when he considers that nature is as responsible for the failure of the farms as the land speculator. Garland complicates his message as he offers a portrait of farm life that refutes an idyllic vision of independent farmers laboring on the land for a comfortable living. His rebuttal of the agrarian fantasy begins to unravel, however, when he assigns blame and identifies reforms in public policy that might result in favorable changes for the farmer. In taking this position, Garland suggests that the possibility of experiencing an idyllic farm life is not entirely fantastic, since the problem is one that could be corrected through social mechanisms. He acknowledges that nature plays a role in the success or failure of the farmer, but he finally suggests that the difficulties created by nature might not lead to disaster if the farmers were not faced with mortgage payments each month, whether or not their crops are successful. Herein Garland reveals that the farm family is caught in the nexus of conflicting forces, in the interplay between nonhuman nature and the human-centered agrarian economy.

Garland undermines his own rebuttal of the agrarian myth with his ambiguous message about correcting social problems. He also undermines his warnings about capricious nature with positive images about the natural features of farm country. The strength of criticism about farming is weakened by a contrasting romantic and sometimes sentimental view of agrarian land—a view that also recognizes the natural beauty inherent in the prairies of the Midwest.

Garland's underlying optimism surfaces in his stories when he creates farmers in "Up the Coulee" who look to the West as a utopia where they might escape the economic realities of Wisconsin and achieve prosperity; it appears again in "Among the Corn Rows" in the figure of Rob, who is actually carving out a prosperous life in the West. This vision recurs throughout Garland's stories and novels of the 1890s, from *Jason Edwards* to *A Little Norsk*. This subtle yet optimistic theme finds a symbolic expression in Garland's romantic panoramic visions of an agricultural garden.[12] Henry Nash Smith has identified how popular discourse of this era described the Midwest as a vast garden—one that embraces a complex of metaphors "expressing fecundity, growth, increase, and blissful labor in the earth" (123) and centers in the frontier farmer. In the early nineteenth century, the garden figured as the symbolic expression of the agrarian dream. When Garland invokes this garden, however, he brings to it a new realistic dimension by placing it in close proximity to squalid farms. This juxtaposition suggests that one may indeed be within view of the other, that the belabored farmer may still enjoy the pleasures of the garden.

Ironically Garland relies on characters who stand at the periph-ery of farm life to confirm that a rich and potentially rewarding connection to nature can indeed be found in the agrarian setting.[13] He seems to argue that an outsider is more capable of observing the natural beauty of the land than a local resident. In "Up the Coulee" and "Among the Corn Rows" Garland frames his images of impoverished farm life with far more appealing scenes that emphasize the beauty of the land. The opening scene of "Up the Coulee" reveals the Wisconsin farm country through the eyes of Howard McLane, the urban actor who experiences the farmland in all of its mythic beauty:[14]

> To lean back in a reclining chair and whirl away in a breezy July day, past lakes, groves of oak, past fields of barley being reaped, past hayfields, where the heavy grass is toppling before the swift sickle, is a panorama of delight, a road full of delicious surprises, where down a sudden vista lakes open, or a distant wooded hill looms darkly blue, or swift streams, foaming deep down the solid rock, send whiffs of cool breezes in at the window. (MTR 54)

Garland implies that if one can pause long enough to "lean back," a wealth of splendid images will manifest themselves. He introduces the importance of leisure in accessing the beauty of the agrarian land—a leisure notably unavailable to overworked farmers. In "Among the Corn Rows" a similarly beautiful landscape is sketched by Seagraves, the journalist. His vision of the land openly invokes the myth of an inexhaustible garden when he sees the prairie scene as "wonderfully beautiful . . . and infinite in reach as a sea" (99). Here, Garland addresses the idea of an agrarian democracy in which farming and freedom are synonymous:

> The faint clouds in the west were getting a superb flame color above and a misty purple below, and the sun had shot them

with lances of yellow light. . . . the sounds of neighboring life began to reach the ear. Children screamed and laughed, and afar off a woman was singing a lullaby. The rattle of wagons and voices of men speaking to their teams multiplied. . . . The whole scene took hold upon Seagraves with irresistible power.

"It is American," he exclaimed. "No other land or time can match this mellow air, this wealth of color, much less the strange social conditions of life on this sunlit Dakota prairie." (100)

Because Seagraves is unencumbered by physical labor, he can recognize the beauty that surrounds them. Rob responds to Seagraves's comments about the landscape, "Landscape be blessed! If you'd been breakin' all day—" (100).

Garland implies what Bailey and Smythe state explicitly when he suggests that the spiritual regeneration that can be derived from the physical beauty of the landscape is usually unrecognized by the farmers and their wives. As Lucretia Burns stoops under the burden of her chores, "She felt vaguely that the night was beautiful. The setting sun, the noise of frogs, the nocturnal insects beginning to pipe" (*OMTR* 82). Lucretia is surrounded by a landscape that offers a spiritual redemption beyond her capacity to perceive. We see this in the scene where she

went out into the garden, which was fragrant and sweet with dew and sun. After picking some berries . . . she sat down on the grass under the row of cottonwoods, and sank into a kind of lethargy. A kingbird chattered and shrieked overhead, the grasshoppers buzzed in the grasses, strange insects with ventriloquist voices sang all about her. (95)

Unlike John Bartram in Crèvecoeur's *Letters*, Lucretia is limited in her ability to appreciate agrarian nature. A perceptual boundary confines her within her deprived existence, denying her the opportunity for the spiritual and emotional regeneration that can be had through an appreciation of the beauty of the land. The

availability of this natural regeneration is defined by the character
of her feminine chores, which generally confine her indoors rather
than putting her out in the field.

Masculine work, which is undertaken out-of-doors, in the fields,
allows for the spiritual and rejuvenating connection to nature. We
see how women can enjoy this connection in "Among the Corn
Rows" in Julia Peterson. When she steps away from the drudgery
of plowing to cool her feet in a stream,

> the beauty of the scene came to her. Over her the wind moved
> the leaves. . . . The river sang with its lips to the pebbles. The
> vast clouds went by majestically, far above the treetops, and the
> snap and buzzing and ringing whir of July insects made a cease-
> less, slumberous undertone of song solvent of all else. The tired
> girl forgot her work. (MTR 109)

In "Among the Corn Rows" Garland describes scenes suggesting
that the beauty of the agrarian landscape offers the possibility of
spiritual transformation to those who work within it. It is that
beauty that sustains Julia until Rob arrives to carry her off to his
Western farm on the plains. Unlike many of the other farmers in
Garland's stories, Julia and Rob can fully appreciate the beauty of
the land and thereby enjoy a spiritual completion and fulfillment
from farm life. For Julia, this may result from her unmarried state.
She is as yet unencumbered by the duties of wife and mother that
will confine her to interior domestic spaces. As Garland concludes
that story, Julia is like Anson and Bert, the bachelor farmers in *A
Little Norsk*. They find remarkable beauty in the same scene that
was hostile and bleak in winter:

> There is no spot more delightful in early April than the sunny
> side of the barn, and Ans and Bert felt this. . . . The eaves were
> dripping, the doves were cooing, the hens singing their harsh-
> throated, weirdly suggestive songs, and the thrilling warmth
> and vitality of the sun and wind of spring made the great, rude
> fellows shudder with a strange delight.

This is a great world—and a great day. I whish't it was always spring. (*MTR* 156)

The land, despite its harsh and hostile qualities, nonetheless seems to promise transformation to those who can survive its tests and can still perceive the beauty and possibilities for spiritual regeneration through a connection to the land. In this moment of nature appreciation, these two characters reveal Garland's naturalism—one that speaks to the influence of nonhuman nature on human experience.

The dream of transformation through a relationship with the land appears most clearly in the character of Rob in "Among the Corn Rows." Garland employs him as a symbol of agrarian optimism, as a character who embodies the image of the wholesome American yeoman farmer, "cheery, wide-awake, good-looking . . . a typical claimholder." Evocative of Whitman's American everyman, Rob is the hardy pioneer of American mythology: "He had dug his own well, built his own shanty, washed and mended his own clothing. He could do anything, and do it well" (*MTR* 101). Rob invokes the myth of self-sufficiency embedded in the agrarian ideal, an ideal that affirms a democracy of small farmers who have shaken off the fetters of Eastern aristocratic landholders. He tells Seagraves, "Well, so I come West, just like a thousand other fellers, to get a start where the cussed European aristocracy hadn't got a hold on the people. . . . I'm my own boss, as I say, an' I'm goin' to *stay* my own boss if I haf to live on crackers" (102).

Rob also figures as a symbol of a larger mythic, democratic agrarian community that reappears throughout Garland's stories. In "God's Ravens" Robert Bloom must return to a rural setting in order to regain his health. He arrives in April, a time suggestive of regeneration, when "Frogs are peeping" and the "smell of spring was in the air" (*MTR* 213). The landscape alone, however, is not adequate to ensure his transformation. He and his wife cannot identify the uplifting qualities of the rural folk, and he becomes progressively weaker. His condition turns, however, when he becomes so ill that he must submit to the ministrations of the community. In his most dejected condition, they rally around him, providing him with sustenance and nurturing that return him to health. The community reveals itself to be fundamentally good. That same goodness is reflected in the Council family of "Under the Lion's Paw," who take in the Haskins and assist them in settling in their farm; and in Widow Gray, in "The Return of the Private," who "was the visible incarnation of hospitality and optimistic poverty" (*MTR* 131).

Garland suggests that although many farmers suffer difficult and impoverished conditions, they nonetheless possess an inherent goodness. He counters a Jeffersonian tenet when he asserts that farm life is degrading and exerts a negative influence over those who engage in farming, but he seemingly confirms that notion when he implies that the farm community provides a positive influence on the nation. Garland may wish to refute the agrarian ideal, but a much stronger affirmation of that ideal appears in his stories. These two contradictory messages demonstrate the tension that most certainly was present for many nineteenth-century Americans who were experiencing, firsthand, the closure of the American frontier and the incumbent hardships created by a land market that favored the speculator and by the agricultural methods that may not have been most conducive to successful farming.

GARLAND'S TENDENCY to promote the cause of the yeoman farmer may have emerged from his own positive memories of farm life as well as from an underlying, though overtly unacknowledged, attachment to the concept of an agrarian society. In 1927 Lucy Hazard suggested that Garland's disenchantment with the lot of farmers was founded in his own early experience with farming. She focuses on Garland's distaste for the agrarian life but hints at his ambivalence on that score when she observes that Garland deals with "the collapse of traditional American idealisms" (264) and argues that Garland's indictment of farming arises in part from "his sense of social injustice under which the farmer labors" (262). In identifying a parallel between "Under the Lion's Paw" and Crèvecoeur's story of Andrew the honest Hebridean, Hazard points to an intentionally ironic element in Garland's stories (264). The ironic component is indeed evident and arises from tensions that exist on several levels in his work.

The most obvious source of irony arises from something I have discussed here and Hazard has suggested: the discrepancy between the reality of agrarian life and the ideal vision of farming that had pervaded American thought well into the twentieth century. Hazard comments on the public response to Garland's stories: "His representation of this life was so marked a departure from the conventional rustic idyl as to call forth a storm of protest at his indictment of farm conditions" (262). Hazard posits that Garland had attacked a belief about the nobility of farming that Americans held dear. That belief was more apparent to Garland's contemporaries such as Hazard, who were inculcated in the agrarian ideal, than to contemporary readers. This irony, therefore, arises from the tension between Garland's textual treatment of the farm theme and popular beliefs surrounding farming, which are never explicated within his texts. It is an irony that arises from the tension between text and context.

Garland also creates a stylistic irony as he draws on two literary styles, juxtaposing a realistic view of agrarian life with a sometimes romantic view of the land itself—a view that arises from his own experience of farming. By adhering to neither style entirely, he becomes a romantic realist, employing realism to address social and economic concerns and employing lyrical romanticism to depict wild and agrarian lands. Garland appears to refute an older vision of American life while simultaneously affirming it, rejecting the idealized model of the hardy, healthy yeoman farmer while confirming the inherent goodness of farming. His place as a realist relies primarily upon his indictment of the agrarian ideal through a realistic depiction of farming. Indeed, his realistic descriptions are forceful if not examined too deeply, and they reveal an aspect of American life that had hitherto been ignored.

Ironically, what finally limits Garland as a realist are his depictions of farm conditions, which ultimately consist of little more than an observation of surfaces. He presents snapshots of squalid agrarian life and directs an accusatory finger at the figure of the land speculator. The social statement embedded in his stories is never developed or supported by substantive argumentation. Garland condemns only an idealized depiction of farming but neither farming itself nor its exalted position in American culture. He counters a superficial idealized view of farming with a superficial realistic view. One must note, however, that his realism extends to his descriptions of nonhuman nature. The nonhuman realm is as breathtakingly beautiful—a source of spiritual inspiration and comfort—as it is simultaneously unpredictable and potentially threatening to human existence.

Garland's shallow realism arises from his failure to examine the agrarian ideal and the conditions that contributed to its formation. The primary assumption upon which he predicates his stories is that farmers are, indeed, the cornerstone of the American democracy. He affirms that the small farm should endure as an American institution. His assumptions are not based on a thoughtful consideration of why the yeoman farmer should survive, why the small farm should endure, or what value that institution brings to the larger society.

Garland's realism falters because of his reductivist tendency to assign a single cause to the failure of the agrarian ideal. He argues that farmers lead impoverished lives solely because of the activity of speculators, while only obliquely informing us of other forces that influence the success of farming. His realism falls short of accurately depicting the complex of influences that shape agriculture and neglects the interplay of other economic forces that are entangled in an agrarian economy: market prices determined by wholesale distributors, the cost of farm implements, and the competitive advantage enjoyed by farmers who possess more sophisticated farming technology. He fails to consider that what might be at fault is not only the extra-agricultural influences but also the participation of the farmers in an agricultural market economy. Garlands's farmers, like Norris's, are not practicing subsistence agriculture but are partners with the very system that destroys them. They willingly buy large tracts of land on credit, essentially gambling that nature and the market will favor them. When either force fails, the farmer—who for market reasons has planted a single crop vulnerable to pestilence and unpredictable weather—is destroyed. Moreover, Garland tends to overlook the regional variations in farming and suggests that the causes for failed farms in the arid Dakotas are the same as those in more humid lands such as Wisconsin and Iowa. While land speculation and taxation figure in both of these areas, the causes for failure depend on other factors as well, such as the arability of the land itself.

Garland implicitly argues for reforms in market conditions that would make land affordable and the small farm successful. His arguments, however, consistently ignore the prevailing economic reality of his time, which is that more people were looking to settle an ever-diminishing frontier and to farm large sections of land for profit rather than a few acres for subsistence. In some works, such as *Jason Edwards*, Garland briefly touches on the crooked land schemes that lured ignorant farmers to lands that could not profitably be farmed. He does not consider that the farmers were, to some extent, victims of their own form of greed, hoping to acquire high-quality land at low prices without inquiring into the actual conditions of that land. Rather than confront that reality, Garland falls back on an emotional appeal based in the idealism he sets out to condemn.

The inconsistencies in Garland's work speak to the very difficult problem of comprehensively describing the way agriculture involves individuals, society, and nature. Emerson grappled with the problem of providing an accurate view of farming, yet he demonstrated that any interpretation of that enterprise depends on and reflects the position of the observer. Throughout Garland's stories we see a similar problem. The farm can be a place of arduous work, and its inhabitants can lead lives as impoverished and bleak as those suffered by the populations of urban tenements. And the farmer can become the victim of unscrupulous speculators. In this scenario the farm and the people who engage in farming are subject to the forces of society. And when such people lack imagination, or the habit of mind to observe the natural world, they may as well live within the confines of urban tenements as on a farm.

Garland also offers the view that the farm is subject to the forces of nature: drought, pestilence, winds, hails, and snow, all shape the success or failure of the agrarian enterprise. Just like those denizens of urban tenements who populate the naturalist fiction of Crane, Norris, and Zola, Garland's farmers are subject to the influences of their natural environment—an environment that is essentially deterministic. Haskins in "Under the Lion's Paw" has no power over the pestilence that drives him to rent a farm, nor does Jason Edwards have control over the hail storm that destroys his wheat crop. Their capacity to exercise their will is ✓ limited by forces over which they have no control.

These limitations are tempered by Garland's own appreciation for the beauty of nature that is found in the agrarian landscape—a beauty that ultimately seems to prevail in such works as *Boy Life on the Prairie*. Garland suggests that despite all of its hardships, farming offers the possibility of an intimate, and indeed positive, spiritual connection to nonhuman nature. He retains a certain optimism derived from a personal knowledge of how satisfying farming can be. Garland creates for his reader the reality of farm ✓ life: it can be as immensely satisfying as it is simultaneously difficult and sometimes disastrous. The most gratifying moments of farming are experienced when a crop makes it to harvest, when nature seemingly cooperates with the farmer, providing rain and sun at the right times, limiting the insects that might decimate a crop. Conversely, the farmer has no power over the negative forces of nature. Garland offers a realistic view of farming when he complicates his discussions with economic issues. Farming is not ✓ simply an idyll, even for the nineteenth-century farmer; it is also a business.

Garland's work is admittedly inconsistent. His fiction is sometimes awkward, his characters wooden, his plots contrived, but his descriptions of the land he loves (is) often lyric. Given the era in which he wrote, and the literary community with whom he wished to associate, he may have felt compelled to create a rationale for writing about the land he loved. *Crumbling Idols* is the legacy of that effort, a statement for a literature that is environmentally centered. This legacy endures most evidently not in his realism but in his romantic attachment to the nonhuman environments of the agrarian scenes he describes, scenes that many critics have interpreted as a condemnation of agrarian life.

The Epic of

California Agriculture

S WE observed in Emerson's "Farming," philosophical considerations of agriculture may find themselves on an uneven conceptual ground, shifting between literal and metaphorical treatments of the subject. The farm can be an actual or a figurative space; farming can be either a physical process related to the husbanding of crops and livestock or a philosophical discipline that brings its practitioner in closer relationship to a spiritual realm of which nonhuman nature is emblematic. For Garland, farming was less complicated; it was primarily a real-world activity rather than a metaphor for social relationships or nonhuman processes. To move from Garland to Norris is to move, once again, to a more abstract treatment of the land. Frank Norris, like Emerson, complicates the idea of the farm. He looks to agriculture as a vehicle for exploring economic and political relationships, in particular the ways that economic interests, such as the railroad monopolies, figured in the lives of "average" Americans—in this case, farmers.[1]

Early in 1899, the twenty-nine-year-old Norris wrote to several friends of his plans to write his epic of wheat. Fired with his own vision, he announced to Harry M. Wright in a letter dated 5 April 1899: "It will be all about the San Joaquin wheat raisers and the

Southern Pacific, and I guess we'll call it The Octopus" (*Letters* 35). According to Franklin Walker, Norris hoped to write a series of novels illustrating the economic forces that were transforming the United States from an agrarian to an industrial society (241). But Norris also suggests in his letter to Harry Wright that his literary ambitions were compelling him toward writing a novel of grand proportions, "the big American novel," one that will possess "the big, Epic, dramatic thing" (*Letters* 35).

Norris conceived his epic while living in New York, far removed from the actual land upon which he would base *The Octopus*. In April of 1899 he traveled west to research the novel, intending to "study the whole thing *on the ground*" in California. As a student of Zola and a proponent of a literature that was founded on an accurate representation of details, Norris was concerned with literary precision and planned to study the subject of his epic from several perspectives.[2] "I mean to do it thoroughly," he wrote, "— get at it from every point of view, the social, agricultural, & political" (*Letters* 35). The plot of the story would center in an actual uprising of farmers that had occurred near Hanford in 1880, but as Walker suggests, Norris had not intended to present the event with historical accuracy (248). Norris, through his commitment to the notion of romance, was more concerned with capturing a quality of life and an accuracy in the spirit of human activities and emotion than in capturing the details of the circumstances and setting of his novel.[3]

The Octopus is a muddle of plots and subplots, a mess of details trivial and significant that seem to defy a coherent reading.[4] The novel focuses on the experience of Presley, a poet who travels to the San Joaquin Valley, where he lingers as a guest of the affluent wheat rancher, Magnus Derrick, and his family. Presley becomes entangled in the battle that pits ranchers Derrick, Annixter, Dyke, and the larger community against the powerful Pacific and Southwestern Railroad. The major action and dominant political statement of the novel emphasizes the extent to which the ranchers were at the mercy of the railroad on which they relied to deliver tools for working their ranches and to take their products to market. The plot centering in the ranchers and the railroad culminates with a great gun fight, in which Annixter and several others are killed. The railroad prevails, but the nefarious railroad agent, S. Behrman, dies, accidentally buried in the cargo hold of a ship under a stream of wheat. Woven into this story are several subplots, including two romances: one between the pragmatic Annixter and the milkmaid Hilma Tree and one between the mysterious Vanamee and his long-dead lover, Angéle. Presley figures as the dramatic witness to the various altercations between the ranchers and the railroad, and throughout, he imagines how he will transform his observations into an epic poem.

Despite Norris's public commitment to the notion of literary accuracy and attention to detail, in *The Octopus* expedience took priority; Norris's plan to quickly complete his novel resulted in some odd incongruities that have made the analysis of the novel both frustrating and challenging. It seems that when reality did not fulfill artistic ends, Norris simply disregarded and redefined his world to suit his project. When Norris traveled to California in √ 1899, wheat was no longer produced in vast farms in the southern San Joaquin Valley; thus he turned to the Santa Anita Rancho in San Benito County for the details surrounding farming. Walker writes that Norris actually "spent little time in the San Joaquin valley in his search for material." Instead, he created his literary setting by "ingeniously transferring a section of San Benito County to the lower San Joaquin, in the process flattening out the hills, enlarging the estates, and moving a Spanish mission over the Coast Range" (248–49). And although Norris was sufficiently concerned with details to travel West to take notes on wheat ranching, he lingered in California for only three months, returning to New York in July to write the actual book (see Pizer, *Novels* 121). He remained in the East throughout the following year and completed *The Octopus* in December of 1900. The first volume of Norris's epic was released to the public in April of 1901 (Walker 272).

Norris was creating a fiction, one that would faithfully represent certain aspects of human experience, but he reveals a strange

✓ blind spot in his notion of literary accuracy as it relates to the environments in which he sets the novel. In addition to transplanting regions, Norris also transplants some fixed and unalterable historical and physical details when he creates a Spanish mission in the region, as well as a seed ranch that was based on the Morse Seed Ranch between San Juan Bautista and Hollister.[5] This seed ranch and the flowers grown there thrive in a region that enjoys the coastal fogs that penetrate inland and maintain summer temperatures many degrees cooler than those in the southern San Joaquin Valley. But while San Benito County enjoys cooling summer fogs, the lower San Joaquin Valley endures chilling winter tule fogs. The seed ranch, as David Wyatt observes, "is an agricultural impossibility in the San Joaquin," while the "coast live oak [had] migrated over the mountains" (97). The naturally occurring plants and animals in each region may overlap, but they
✓ also differ. These facts are irrelevant to Norris, however, whose primary concern is human activity. This literary act holds real-world consequences to the extent that it reflects a significant neglect of the unique characteristics of various regions.[6]

These rather liberal authorial acts reflect the primary concern of Norris's literary project, which is to employ the various entities of the scenes he draws as symbolic elements within his larger epic. In *The Octopus* the land itself is significant only as the place in which Norris sets his story. Norris privileges the human relationships in his novel, while the land on which the action plays out, including the agricultural land, is intended to offer textual messages to the reader, without necessarily actually representing the land itself. Unlike Emerson, who considers that the nonhuman environment might be regarded for both its actual and its imag-
✓ inative dimensions, Norris looks to the land exclusively as the set on which he unfolds his epic.

In transplanting regions, Norris suggests that environmentally, one region is like another, that land itself matters less than the dramas enacted by people on this land. This transplanting might seem relatively benign when we consider that its realm is fiction, but as Joseph Meeker has observed, our literature provides us with models that influence our perceptions of the nonhuman world as well as our responses to it (8). Literary acts are derived from observations and perceptions of the world; moreover, a text can influence and shape the perceptions and behaviors of its readers. We might argue that Norris's tendency to elide the nonhuman realm in the interest of literary drama may be inconsequential to the larger art in whose service Norris commits these acts, yet such acts take on more ominous consequences when this practice is transferred to nonliterary, actual-world behaviors. The consequences of applying literary devices to nonliterary subjects will be evident later in my discussion of William Smythe.

In defining the scope of *The Octopus*, Norris ostensibly limits his subjects to the social, or the relationships among humans; the agricultural, or the relationships between humans and their cultivation of crops; and the political, the relationships between humans and their governing institutions. In his early letters to friends and acquaintances, Norris suggests that he will move away from his quirky preoccupation with character study and psychological motivation, which figured at the center of *McTeague*, and write a novel that addresses weightier themes. Indeed, he will include character studies of key figures, such as Presley, Magnus Derrick, Buck Annixter, and Vanamee, but they prove emblematic; they are types that provide us with clues about the various ways humans might relate to the land, to other humans, and to the great amorphous entity Norris speaks of as "force." Although Norris includes the theme of agriculture in his grand plan, farming finally figures only as an activity that illustrates a larger conflict between competing human forces, both social and political. The agricultural land of *The Octopus* provides a mediating ground between the force of raw nature and the force inherent in humans and their institutions.[7]

Norris invests a greater attention to the social and political contexts of agriculture than to agriculture itself, but he does reveal an awareness of the factors that were influencing agriculture and its practice in the late years of the nineteenth century. Norris employs the theme of agriculture to illustrate a larger and more significant philosophical concern, enriching that discussion through his development of five central characters who embody a range of attitudes about the land that reflect on larger popular discussions related to agricultural practice and nature appreciation. Presley represents the intellectual aesthete; Derrick and Dyke represent the entrepreneur; Annixter, the progressive science-based agrarian; and Vanamee, the mystic wanderer and nature lover.[8] Norris's characterizations tap into the paradox that is at the heart of debates about the relationships between humans and the nonhuman world that emerged with the rise of technology. If humans are inherently animals—that is, *of* nature—then our creations, whether they be burrows, digging sticks, plows, or engines, are inherently "natural" as well.[9] Norris suggests this paradox in *The Octopus* through the various attitudes of his characters and the three linking but oddly conflicting metaphors that dominate the novel: the wheat, the locomotive, and the octopus.

IN CREATING his epic of the wheat, Norris hoped to use the agricultural and political themes to convey a philosophical concept that centers in the notion of force, but his management of these wide-ranging elements—in particular, his use of wheat, the railroad, and the locomotive—lacks coherent explication. Norris envisions the wheat as a force, imbuing it with the manifold cultural associations embedded in such a symbolic entity: it figures as a material manifestation of biological energy, the source of human sustenance, and a manifestation of human wealth. Conversely Norris also turns to the railroad to represent the concept of force, using the locomotive, with its "enormous eye, cyclopean, red," as a symbol of the railroad's unfeeling power. The locomotive suggests that the railroad's strength is, at least in part, derived from its technological associations, since the engine is a product of human technology. But Norris also invokes the peculiar image of an octopus lurking beneath the earth to symbolize the vast and insidious influence of the railroad. This symbol unites and confounds his symbols of the wheat and the locomotive: the octopus is a nonhuman entity residing within the nonhuman realm of nature. Norris, however, places this octopus within the earth rather than the ocean—which suggests that this natural creature is unnatural, living outside of its native aquatic environment, somewhere beneath the surface of the San Joaquin Valley.

In drawing together these symbols—the wheat, the locomotive, and the earth-octopus—Norris illustrates the interplay of force and its influence on humans. His efforts at demonstrating the complex relationship between human and nonhuman entities is clumsy at best and suggests that he did not approach the topic with a clear understanding of either the concepts he was invoking or the larger message he hoped to promote. The end result, however, is rather interesting because he ultimately reveals the complexity and interrelatedness of these categories and the fact that one cannot neatly extract human activity from some notion of a larger amorphous nature.

Woven into his commentary on force is the narrative surrounding agriculture; Norris obviously intends that we draw some conclusions about the activities in which the ranchers engage. Joseph McElrath argues that Norris describes the ranchers as "profit-oriented individuals who exercise absolute power over their ranch hands." They are like the "businessmen who abuse them." Norris, he suggests, depicts ranchers not as "noble husbandmen of the soil" but as "agri-businessmen struggling to prevail in a dog-eat-dog economic order" (92). I contend that Norris's attention to the rise of agriculture in California speaks to a larger awareness of the changing shape of agriculture nationwide. McElrath's reading points to Norris's efforts to introduce parallels between the ranchers and the railroad magnates; as businessmen none is more guilty than another. Indeed, they are similarly motivated by profit and, toward that end, are exercising force on the environment through the manipulation of the wheat. Moreover, both groups are simultaneously subject to larger forces: the ranchers are subject to the force of the railroads, and the railroads are subject to the larger and amorphous universal force. Neither the ranchers nor the railroads operate autonomously.

Norris's analysis of the agricultural issues is oddly incomplete, however, and is simultaneously entangled with his attention to the theme of force, which is itself tangled with his notions of nature. Norris hardly seems aware of the various categories he draws into textual play. While Emerson provided his readers with an early definition of nature's two expressions, Norris leaves us with a collection of implied and often muddled definitions. Emerson, drawing on the ideas of Immanuel Kant, posited nature as the "me" and the "not me." He recognized the fundamental conflicts between philosophical definitions of nature and popular, or common, definitions; thus he informed his readers that he would be addressing nature in its philosophical dimensions—that is, considering nature to be all-encompassing and inclusive of humans— except when he spoke of it in its common definition as the terrestrial manifestations of all that is nonhuman. Norris, in contrast, offers us little help in this area; he implies rather than explicates.[10] He speaks of force as manifested in terrestrial life—in certain elements of nonhuman nature, such as the wheat. At other moments he conflates nature and force. The closest we have to an explanation of nature comes late in the novel as Presley speaks with the railroad magnate Shelgrim and considers the implications of the grand shoot-out at which Annixter and his friends died:

> there was no malevolence in nature. Colossal indifference only, a vast trend toward appointed goals. Nature was, then, a gigantic engine, a vast cyclopean power, huge, terrible, a leviathan with a heart of steel, knowing no compunction, no forgiveness, no tolerance; crushing out the human atom standing in its way with nirvanic calm, the agony of destruction sending never a jar, never the faintest tremor through all that prodigious mechanism of wheels and cogs. (406)

Norris suggests that nature *is* technology or, at least, is embedded in technology. This strange and horrible energy he invokes drives all of creation; however, it also drives human invention and, in fact, is manifested in the machines created by humans—and, through extension, by the political and economic systems that they use, in turn, to dominate the human and nonhuman worlds.[11] Norris characterizes nature as a driving force, yet it also possesses a distinctly organic character, existing not just as an abstract energy but also as a physical entity that variously appears as the influence of environment in humans themselves and in the coequal symbol of force, the earth-octopus.

Norris establishes a tautology, defining nature as driving force and defining force as an abstract entity driving all of creation, existing independent of human control and without human values such as justice, empathy, or mercy. Nature operates like a vast machine and is reducible to power alone:

> Men were naught, death was naught, life was naught; FORCE only existed—FORCE that brought men into the world, FORCE that crowded them out of it to make way for the succeeding generation, FORCE that made the wheat grow, FORCE that garnered it from the soil to give place to the succeeding crop.
>
> It was the mystery of creation, the stupendous miracle of recreation; the vast rhythm of the seasons, measured, alternative, the sun and the stars keeping time as the eternal symphony of reproduction swung in its tremendous cadences like the colossal pendulum of an almighty machine—primordial energy flung out from the hand of the Lord God himself, immortal, calm, infinitely strong. (446)

Force ultimately drives nature. The physical manifestation of this force is the wheat, which drives rancher and railroad magnate alike. Norris invokes a metaphor reminiscent of Emerson as he identifies nature as a perfectly timed machine whose end product is the wheat. The wheat ranch is synonymous with the force of nature, which is conflated with the railroad. At a climactic moment as the ranchers realize they are at the mercy of the railroad, Norris lapses into a consideration of the wheat, effectively suggesting that the force of the railroad and the force of the wheat are one:

As if human agency could affect this colossal power! What were these heated, tiny squabbles, this feverish insect, to the great, majestic, silent ocean of the wheat itself! Indifferent, gigantic, resistless, it moved in its appointed grooves. Men, Lilliputians, gnats in the sunshine, buzzed impudently in their tiny battles, were born, lived through their little day, died, and were forgotten; while the wheat, wrapped in nirvanic calm, grew steadily under the night, alone with the stars and with God. (316)

Donald Pizer argues for a coherence in Norris's vision, suggesting that "the cycle of the wheat's growth is an epitome of the divine energy or force present in nature and in all natural processes" (*Novels* 127). This interpretation might hold, were it not for the fact that the wheat is hardly a product of nonhuman nature alone. Ironically Norris neglects in this passage a significant circumstance surrounding the existence of the wheat, one that he acknowledges elsewhere. The wheat does not emerge spontaneously from the soil; it grows in the San Joaquin Valley through a complex relationship between human activity and the "force" of nonhuman nature. Wheat is neither native to the region nor well-adapted to it. Even the farmers whom Norris portrays have been engaged in a sophisticated process of seed selection, seeking to maximize their yields. We learn from Harran Derrick that they should "stay by the White Sonora and Propo" because, as a workman observes, the red Clawson seed did not yield "a very good catch" (45). Norris is aware that the plantings of the farmers are selected for specific reasons, and if the wheat harvest is successful, the bounty exists as much through human force and design as through the force of nature.

This confusion about the categories of natural and unnatural and the relationships among them is also reflected in Norris's inclusion of the irrigation ditch early in the novel. We are told that the ditch creates a line that divides properties; later it provides the ranchers refuge during their showdown with the railroad. The ditch also figures within the larger question about the relationship between humans and nature and holds broader implications from an agricultural perspective. Norris describes the irrigation ditch, which was still under construction, as a "natural boundary between two divisions of the Los Muertos ranch" (17). The ditch, which has been created to carry water onto an arid land, is deemed as natural. That judgment may seem paradoxical, but it might also suggest that Norris regards human interventions on the land as natural—perhaps a reasonable expression of our efforts to survive. This interpretation would shift all the larger human activity, especially that which is technologically based, into the realm of the natural—which is, in turn, a category that figures within the still greater realm of force.

NORRIS'S EFFORT at explicating the relationships among humans, nature, and force finds a more comprehensible expression in his development of his major characters. In developing the players in his epic and situating them within the setting of *The Octopus*, Norris provides several examples for the various ways that humans may situate themselves within the dynamic flow of nature and force. Their actions occur on actual land. Their real-world behaviors hold tangible consequences; thus Norris's strangely abstract explication of the interconnections among humans, nature, and force is made more comprehensible in the various subplots surrounding the different characters.

As *The Octopus* opens, we observe Presley bicycling across an arid, dust-clogged land where the prevailing image is the sun: "all the vast reaches of the San Joaquin Valley . . . was bone-dry, parched, and baked and crisped after four months of cloudless weather, when the day seemed always at noon, and the sun blazed white-hot over the valley" (9–10). Norris provides us with little evidence of nonhuman nature. Vegetation is almost nonexistent; our first sight of plant life is a "few flower beds and [a] grove of eucalyptus trees" that surrounds the Derrick ranch house (12). At a distance a "live oak" is visible. The wheat fields are "dirty yellow" stubble, suggesting an absence of wheat rather than the presence of earth. Wyatt considers Norris's description of the Valley as a "space distinctive in its vacancy" (108). Indeed, as Presley gazes to the south, he observes not a biologically diverse nonhuman environment, or even a biologically cultured landscape, but human efforts at defining space through boundaries that suggest ownership: Derrick's property is defined by "the line of wire fence that separated it from the third division; and to the north, seen faint and blue through the haze and shimmer of the noon sun, a long file of telegraph poles showed the line of the railroad and marked Derrick's northeast boundary" (16). Presley reads the marks imposed by humans, seeing the land only as a text where these signs impart meaning about the relationships among the people who inhabit the land.

If there is a "natural" dimension to this agricultural land, we are offered little visual evidence of it through Presley's eyes. Instead, Norris emphasizes Presley's perceptual framework for valuing the land and its elements. Time has halted: "It was the period between seasons when nothing was being done, when the natural forces seemed to hang suspended. There was no rain, there was no wind, there was no growth, no life; the very stubble had no force even to rot. The sun alone moved" (16). This great agricultural land, ironically, lacks all life after the harvest—a perspective that describes a metaphorical rather than an actual condition of farmland.

Presley, as the observing artist, enjoys access to the many landscapes of *The Octopus*, but we often find him gazing on a scene, enjoying a panorama in which the topographical and biological features of the land have been abstracted into symbolic components. Through Presley, Norris reveals one dimension of his own literary project: the land will be considered for its aesthetic potential. Early in the novel, before the action between ranchers and railroad unfolds, Presley climbs to a promontory at the headwaters of Broderson Creek, above the Valley. From that point, he gazes immediately below him and identifies the Mission and the Seed ranch, Annixter's ranch house, the town of Guadalajara, and the eucalyptus and poplar trees marking Derrick's land and the county road. Presley quickly discounts what he observes, however, as little more than elements in an aesthetic assemblage:

But all this seemed to be only foreground, a mere array of accessories—a mass of irrelevant details. Beyond Annixter's, beyond Guadalajara, beyond the Lower Road, beyond Broderson Creek, on to the south and west, infinite, illimitable, stretching out there under the sheen of the sunset forever and forever, flat, vast, unbroken, a huge scroll, unrolling between the horizons. . . . (39)

Norris suggests that the land on which his great epic will be enacted is incidental to his story rather than central to it. The physical features of the land—both those created by humans and the natural nonhuman features—figure only as foreground, while the larger California land where the dramatic events will unfold represents the surface on which the epic will be inscribed. Given this declaration early in the novel, it is evident why Norris falters in his accuracy with regard to the details of the nonhuman physical environment.

Presley is an aesthete, experiencing the land almost entirely as an abstraction. He exists in a temporal parallax, seemingly incapable of perceiving in any given discrete moment the land around him. Instead, he interprets the land through layers of literary history, "as Homer saw, as Beowulf saw." Presley understands that "life is here . . . the poem is here; . . . here under our hands, in the desert, in the mountain, on the ranch," but he equates the life he lives with poetry. Reality resides under his hand, which will transform ideas into language. Vanamee recognizes Presley's tendency to abstract the world, to transform it into language that mediates his experience. "But why write?" Vanamee asks him; "Why not *live* in it?" (35). Presley, however, cannot imagine an immediate, intimate, experience of nature similar to that which Vanamee embraces:

"No, I could not do that," declared Presley. "I want to go back, but not so far as you. I feel that I must compromise. I must find expression. I could not lose myself like that in your desert. When its vastness overwhelmed me, or its beauty dazzled me, or its loneliness weighed down upon me, I should have to record my impressions. Otherwise I should suffocate. (36)

While the deserts of the Southwest and the "primordial" wilderness of which Vanamee speaks are too horrible for Presley to experience without the mediation of language, Presley apparently can enjoy moments of serenity in the relatively tame lands surrounding the wheat ranches. Among the oak trees of the foothills, he finds a comfortable perch where he listens to the "prolonged murmur of the spring and creek." There, "the sense of his own personality became blunted . . . consciousness dwindled to a point, the animal in him stretched itself, purring" (37). The poet realizes a moment of serenity within the realm of nonhuman nature, yet even in semiconsciousness Presley's language-bound mind transforms his experience into metaphor as he finds himself "lapsing back to the state of the faun, the satyr" (38).[12] He cannot simply experience the glade for what is actually there—for the trees, the grass, the creek, and possibly, the animals that populate it. Instead, his experience here when he pauses to rest is mediated by language, by an interpretation not even his own but one that emerges from the mythology of another era and another land. Presley is hopelessly alienated from the terrestrial realm by his own tendency to translate experience into text. As he experiences the land, he selectively acknowledges certain of its elements while ignoring others and thereby reinscribes the scene, creating one that conforms to his memory of mythology rather than actually describing what is before him. He writes not of California but of ancient Greece and Rome.

The various landscapes Presley observes throughout *The Octopus* become increasingly abstracted as his epic takes form. When Presley returns to the San Joaquin Valley after the massacre at the irrigation ditch and his visit to Shelgrim, he moves through the landscape of the repossessed ranchos and pauses as he nears the headwaters of Broderson Creek. There he gazes back on the Valley and on the same view he has observed early in the novel:

The whole gigantic sweep of the San Joaquin expanded titanic before the eye of the mind, flagellated with heat, quivering and shimmering under the sun's red eye. It was the season after the harvest, and the great earth, the mother, after its period of reproduction, its pains of labor, delivered of the fruit of its loins, slept the sleep of exhaustion in the infinite repose of the colossus, benignant, eternal, strong, the nourisher of nations, the feeder of an entire world. (446)

The boundaries among the various spaces, which he had observed the previous fall, are erased; the arbitrary borders that distinguish human property are subsumed into a space dominated by an anthropomorphic mother nature. All evidence of human presence has disappeared. Norris's allusion to Titans, harvest, and civilizations offers little information about the actual human or nonhuman sights Presley observes. The property lines that have figured in the battles are not visible; neither are the ranch buildings, the roads, the towns, or the fences. In fact Norris provides us with no image that might actually reflect the San Joaquin Valley. We see only a searing sun. The enduring sensory image is one of red light. The land itself has effectively disappeared as Presley, absorbed in his human concerns, reflects on the text he will create.

Presley is no oddity in his tendency to selectively focus on certain features of his environment with the goal of textually rendering those features as art. His capacity for abstracting environmental entities is shared by many other characters whose purposes are not aesthetic and whose actions carry greater consequences in Norris's realm of force. Presley's perceptions shape his art; Derrick and Dyke perceive the land in a way that shapes its physical alteration. For them, the land is not an object of aesthetic interpretation but an economic resource from which they will extract wealth through the cultivation of wheat and hops.

Magnus Derrick is a maverick rancher. His relationship with the earth has a historic dimension; farming represents only his most recent effort at exploiting the land for quick wealth. Derrick had arrived in California decades earlier, realizing success in mining during the gold rush. When the gold strikes disappeared, he turned to the next gold rush and enjoyed the early boom in California wheat:

> He had been as lucky in his mines as in his gambling, sinking shafts and tunneling in violation of expert theory and finding "pay" in every case. Without knowing it, he allowed himself to work his ranch much as if he were still working his mine. The old-time spirit of '49, haphazard, unscientific, persisted in his mind. Everything was a gamble—who took the greatest chances was most apt to be the greatest winner. (51)

Derrick is a "type," the sort of farmer of whom agrarians such as Liberty Hyde Bailey would be critical. He perceives the land as a resource for commercial exploitation. One may drill holes in the earth to extract minerals, or one might drill holes to plant seeds, which will yield a different sort of wealth.[13] For Derrick, the means by which he extracts wealth from the earth is of little concern, but within the larger symbolic scheme of the novel, Derrick's prior history as a miner is significant. He understands both the task of extracting wealth from the earth and the way the materials he extracts figure in the larger economy. Moreover, as a miner, he possesses a symbolic understanding of subterranean processes. This fact will become meaningful when Norris develops his incongruous metaphor of the earth-octopus that lurks beneath the surface of the agricultural land.

Norris provides us with an alternative to Derrick's style of farming through the character of Annie Derrick, Magnus's wife. Uncomfortable with the large-scale farming in which her husband is involved, she reflects an Eastern sensibility about the farm and its place in the community. Embracing an idealized agrarianism, she takes her notion of a farm from the Ohio landscape of her girlhood, where farmers engaged in the husbanding of diverse crops and stock:

five hundred acres neatly partitioned into the water lot, the cow pasture, the corn lot, the barley field, and wheat farm; cozy, comfortable, homelike; where the farmers loved the land, caressing it, coaxing it, nourishing it as though it were a thing almost conscious; where the seed was sowed by hand, and a single two-horse plow was sufficient for the entire farm; where the scythe sufficed to cut the harvest, and the grain was thrashed with flails. (48)

Norris describes a self-sustaining family farm, one that integrates the many components of agrarian life. The farmer raises the grain on which he fattens his stock and feeds his family. He likely also raises his own food supply and trades only the small surpluses. Annie Derrick is horrified at the spectacle of her husband's agriculture, which is "almost unnatural." She is disturbed by the heavy equipment, which "bullied into a yield of three hundred and fifty thousand bushels." If she is disturbed by these methods, she is equally troubled by the effect of such farming techniques on the aesthetics of the space, which has become a visual monoculture: "The direct brutality of ten thousand acres of wheat, nothing but wheat as far as the eye could see, stunned her a little" (48). Through her own approach to farming as an enterprise directed toward human subsistence rather than profit, Annie Derrick illustrates a sensitivity to the land that is lacking in her husband. Norris's female characters, simply through their gender, enjoy a √ greater affinity with the maternal earth than do the male characters. It is no mistake, in other words, that Annie is closer to the earth than ranchers like Magnus, who work the land for monetary gain.

While Magnus Derrick exemplifies the entrepreneur who rides the crest of the first wave of money-makers, Dyke exemplifies the Johnny-come-lately who hopes to realize the prosperity enjoyed by the large-scale ranchers who had begun their enterprises a few years earlier. Like Magnus, Dyke has no background in farming; however, unlike him, Dyke is no businessman but a locomotive engineer who was fired from the P. and S. W. Railroad for demanding a fair wage for his lengthy service. Norris foreshadows Dyke's fate when Dyke complains to Presley about the circumstances that surrounded his dismissal: "I went to the General Office and ate dirt" (20). Indeed, Dyke will eat even more dirt before the novel concludes and he finds himself with a ruined farm and a jail sentence.

Dyke is strangely naive, a hard-working railroad man who hopes to create a new livelihood in a farming enterprise with his brother. Unlike Magnus Derrick or Annixter, Dyke is a small-time farmer; he plans to raise hops on a mere five hundred acres—land on which his brother has "an option" (19). Farming is a business enterprise, and Dyke is confident that he can be as competent at farming as he has been at train engineering. The determining factor for his entering into the project is potential income: "My brother and I will take up this hop ranch. . . . there ought to be money in hops" (20). Harran Derrick affirms this view, bringing in the aspect of the global marketplace: "The crop in Germany and in New York has been a dead failure for the last three years . . . there's likely to be a shortage and a stiff advance in the price. . . . Sure, hops ought to be a good thing" (57).

Dyke's plan to enter hop farming is a business decision, yet he lacks the necessary background to make an informed business or farming decision. He is a locomotive engineer whose understanding of the world has been shaped by his experience of machines, which operate according to a discernible and predictable order. Dyke infuses his mechanistic apprehension of reality with a governing principle that is ethical in its basis. He defines order in terms of human values such as honor and fairness and thus is outraged when the railroad dismisses him for demanding a fair wage. He seems not to recognize that the order governing the railroad is economic and that its ethos is defined by the principle of maximizing profit. If he had understood the principles governing the railroad barons, he would have recognized a logic in their decisions and anticipated their actions.

Despite Dyke's prior experience, which revealed that the P. and S. W. did not operate fairly, he nonetheless believes in a larger ethic of honor and expects that the railroads will abide by their word when it comes to setting their rate tariffs for shipping his crop. He says of the railroad agent, S. Behrman, "business is business, and he would have to stand by a contract in black and white" (57). Not only does Dyke bring a notion of honor to his interpretation of his experience; he "grounds" his experience in language. Later, when the railroad rescinds that contract, they present Dyke with a new rate schedule: "It was inscribed at the top 'Tariff Schedule No. 8,' and underneath these words, in brackets, was a smaller inscription, '*Supersedes No. 7 of Aug. 1*'" (245). Dyke has disregarded what he knows to be true—that the railroads operate logically according to a profit ethic—for the promise of possibilities that were suggested by the words on the page. He believed that language would bind the railroad to honorable behavior. Like ✓ Presley, whose experience of the world is always mediated by language, Dyke finally grounds his reality in words rather than experience.

Norris sets Dyke apart from the other ranchers through his peculiar naïveté and further differentiates him from the other ranchers in his unique choice in crops. While Derrick, Annixter, and the other ranchers are, through the cultivation of wheat, "the nourishers of nations" (458), Dyke raises a crop whose only value is in brewing beer. Throughout *The Octopus* Norris invests the wheat with considerable symbolic weight as the source of sustenance and the ineluctable force of nature; thus, in creating Dyke as a farmer of hops, he suggests a contrasting symbolism, implying that Dyke may have faltered not only in his "reading" of the nature of the railroad but also in his choice of crops. As plants that can offer little nourishment, hops operate symbolically outside of the larger organic harmony sustained by the wheat. The discordant dimension of Dyke's choice appears in the character of Dyke's hop fields, which are defined by a "bewildering, innumerable multitude of poles, connected with a maze of wire and twine" that form a "bare forest" (157). When spring arrives, his fields become an unnatural island of green, a veritable "forest of green hops" (240) that seems to be the only mark of green on the Valley farmland.[14] Norris suggests a fundamental paradox in this choice of crops, which Dyke raises despite the fact that he "was a strictly temperate man" (242). That he later lapses into dipsomania further underscores the irony.

Dyke fails to anticipate the force of free enterprise as manifested in the railroad's activities and the extent to which hop farming will be implicated in the larger commercial structure. Yet he can hardly be expected to understand how agriculture will figure in the larger network of force. Dyke's life has been immersed in technology; he understood the world through the cab of a locomotive. His vision is tuned to identifying nature only where it intersects with technology or when it is framed by the cab of a locomotive window. Dyke lacks a knowledge of and experience with nonhuman nature; consequently, he can neither recognize nor defend himself against the octopus, the "natural" counterpart of the locomotive, which resides underground, beyond technology:

> Under his feet the ground seemed mined; down there below him in the dark the huge tentacles went silently twisting and advancing, spreading out in every direction, sapping the strength of all opposition, quiet, gradual, biding the time to reach up and out and grip with a sudden unleashing of gigantic strength. (244)

Dyke becomes aware of this subterranean entity only when his well-being is threatened and he cannot possibly formulate a defense. He has hitherto ignored the cautions of farmers, men who understand the earth as well as the long reach of the octopus.

Dyke's downfall results from his ignorance; his experience causes him to misjudge his situation. Believing that force is embedded and contained only in the technological symbols of the railroad, he cannot perceive the terrestrial symbol of force, even when he has been warned about it. Finally, when he does recognize it, he cannot retaliate. The octopus reaches at him "from below, from out the dark beneath his feet, coiling around his throat, throttling him, strangling him, sucking his blood. For a moment he thought of the courts, but instantly laughed at the idea. What court was immune from the power of the monster?" (249). The monster is the force of nature itself, conflated with the railroads. In this moment Dyke recognizes the meaninglessness of language, of the rate tariffs on which his future has been based, and of the laws in whose text the court's power resides.

The earth-octopus transcends social structure and operates outside of the ethical order of human honor. Dyke, as an engineer, cannot identify the disorder or unpredictability that is inherent within "natural" systems. Magnus Derrick has worked as a miner, *under ground*, and is therefore aware of the symbolic business that lurks within the earth, in nature. Derrick can also anticipate the problems that will be posed by the railroads and makes a valiant effort to avoid and overcome them. In contrast, Dyke is effectively sideswiped, unable even to anticipate his fate. When his ruin comes, both the cause and the result are manifested in his farm itself: "Weeds were already choking the vines. Everywhere the poles sagged and drooped. Many had even fallen, dragging the vines with them, spreading them over the ground in an inextricable tangle of dead leaves, decaying tendrils, and snarled string" (280). The octopus, which symbolizes the control of the railroad, becomes physically evident in the tangle mass of dying hops that is Dyke's farm.

Norris underscores the significance of Dyke's discordant choices and failed vision in his career shift from locomotive engineer to farmer. Throughout the novel he identifies Dyke not as a farmer but as a "discharged engineer" (142), a "former engineer" (157), and an "ex-engineer" (247, 250–51). Like Derrick, Dyke has turned to this livelihood after a failure in other activities, but unlike Derrick, he is an inexperienced businessman. Moreover, Derrick has a prior association with the earth through his experience as a miner, while Dyke's only prior association is as a driver of engines, an agent of the octopus. Dyke lacks knowledge of farming and must rely on the expertise of "a foreman who knows all about hops" (142). Norris reinforces this inferior condition when Dyke discovers that he too has been ruined by the railroad

through an unanticipated increase in shipping rates: "The working man turned farmer! What a target for jeers—he who had
fancied he could elude the railroad!" (247). As an engineer, he can
understand neither the nature of farming nor the nature of the
railroad.

Magnus Derrick and Dyke contrast with Annixter, who represents a new breed of farmer. Annixter distinguishes himself from
the other wheat ranchers in the way that he considers his land as
more than an agricultural mine from which he will extract a finite
body of resources. Annixter is a wise farmer who enjoys a college
education in disciplines that reflect the new era of agriculture:
"finance, political economy, and scientific agriculture." This education has imbued Annixter with an appreciation for the land and,
perhaps, a greater personal commitment to his role as its steward.
He practices a form of agriculture that is sustainable: rather than
burn his wheat stubble, he sells grazing rights to sheep herders,
who graze their flocks on refuse that might otherwise be burned,
and in the process he "also manures his land as the sheep move
from place to place" (23). Annixter is aware of the negative environmental effects that are created by the agricultural practices
of such folks as Magnus Derrick: " 'That's right, there's your western farmer,' he exclaimed contemptuously. 'Get the guts out of
your land; work it to death; never give it a rest. Never alternate
your crop, and then when your soil is exhausted, sit down and roar
about hard times' " (26). Intending to work his land in perpetu-
ity, Annixter contrasts with farmers like Derrick, who will raise
wheat until the soil will yield no more.[15]

Annixter appreciates nonhuman nature, even as he embraces
technology in his farming. His bedroom is decorated with "a bunch
of herbs or flowers, lamentably withered and gray with dust . . . and
a yellowed photograph of Annixter's combined harvester" (117).
His college diploma, evidence of his mastery of scientific agriculture, also graces a wall. Although Annixter is concerned with
raising wheat, he nonetheless has an aesthetic appreciation for the
natural beauty of the region. As he sets out to begin his workday, he
observes the scene: the Coast Range and the Sierras as they "stood

out pale amethyst against the delicate pink and white sheen of the horizon. The sunlight was a veritable flood, crystal, limpid, sparkling, setting a feeling of gaiety in the air, stirring up an effervescence in the blood" (120). Unlike Presley, who must remove himself from the farmland to see the beauty of the region as a panorama, Annixter can pause in the midst of his farm yard, and see the larger world from all sides. Even as he retires for the night, he envisions the land, bringing together his appreciation for nature with his understanding of farming and cultivation:

> Then, at the end of all, it was the ranch again, seen in a last brief glance before he had gone to bed; the fecundated earth, calm at last, nursing the implanted germ of life, ruddy with the sunset, the horizons purple. . . . The barn fowls were roosting in the trees near the stable, the horses crunching their fodder in the stalls. (152)

Annixter does not distinguish between the nature of the greater countryside and the nature of the farm. The distant mountains surrounding the farm possess a beauty that is not more impressive than the beauty to be enjoyed in the earth he has sown, in the birds that inhabit his barn yard, or even in the horses, which he employs to help plow his fields.

Norris encourages us to conflate Annixter's appreciation for nature and the land with his appreciation and affection for Hilma Tree. Through Annixter's relationship with Hilma, we observe his emerging awareness to his own animal nature. Hilma's surname alone suggests that Norris intends for us to identify her as providing a conduit to the nonhuman realm. Indeed Norris may be specifically invoking a pagan myth related to sexuality and nature: Hilma Tree is a California Daphne sought by Annixter's Apollo.[16] Norris also invokes some rather obvious images surrounding Hilma to encourage us to identify her as a conduit to a maternal earth. She is a milkmaid—a role directly relating her to the stuff that gives life—who seems to straddle the world of humans and animals: "There was a certain generous amplitude to the full, round curves of her hips and shoulders that suggested the pre-cocious maturity of a healthy vigorous animal life passed under the hot southern sun of a half-tropical country" (64). Yet despite her "warm-blooded" animalism, Hilma is nonetheless innocent and pure, "clean and feminine"; in her "the natural, intuitive refinement of the woman [was] not as yet defiled and crushed out" (65). Norris abstracts women into symbols of a greater nature. Hilma provides us with insights about Annixter; in a world in which perception is androcentric, Hilma and nature are conflated, merely entities through whom Annixter discovers his own divine spirit.

Pizer explores Annixter's transformation from misanthrope to tender loving husband and neighbor through his love for Hilma Tree (see *Novels* 127–33). Annixter realizes his love at the mo-ment when he sees the new spring wheat sprouting from the land. After a night of heartfelt soul-searching about Hilma, Annixter watches the sun rise over the Valley and realizes that the wheat has sprouted:

> The wheat had come up. It was there before him, around him, everywhere, illimitable, immeasurable. The winter brownness of the ground was overlaid with a little shimmer of green. The promise of the sowing was being fulfilled. The earth, the loyal mother, who never failed, who never disappointed was keeping her faith. . . . Once more the Titan, benignant, calm, stirred and woke, and the morning abruptly blazed into glory upon the spectacle of a man whose heart leaped exuberant with the love of a woman. (260)

Annixter experiences an epiphany when he relates his under-standing of how nature works to his spirituality and his love for Hilma.[17] In practicing scientific agriculture, he was familiar with the relationship between farming practices and crop yields, and when he extends his notion of "husbanding" from the land to his human relationships, he realizes a spiritual transformation. If there is some relationship between the way the land is farmed and what it "gives" to humans, then that same concept of reciprocity may extend to human relationships. When Annixter grasps this concept, Hilma agrees to marry him. It may be an ironic and cynical statement by Norris that Annixter, the one rancher who practices an agriculture that might be in harmony with nature, is denied even the pathetic survival granted Derrick and Dyke.

Annixter is somewhat closer to nonhuman nature than Derrick, but the one who comes the closest to it is the enigmatic Vanamee. Like Annixter, Vanamee has a college education, but his life has followed the bizarre path defined by his early love for the mythic Angéle.[18] Blessed with telepathy, he seems to inhabit a world that exists primarily within himself. Norris informs us throughout the novel that Vanamee lives close to nature, but the character is also distinctive for the way that he has traveled and has been a mysterious "dweller in the wilderness" through his lengthy explorations (154). He has traveled through the Southwest, Mexico, the states of Utah and Nevada, and the mountains of California, and we are to understand that his solitary excursions place him in closer proximity to nonhuman nature and its forces. Vanamee explains to Presley the relationship between his telepathy and his interactions with nature:

People who live much alone and close to nature experience the sensation of it. Perhaps it is something fundamental we share with plants and animals. The same thing that sends the birds south long before the first colds, the same thing that makes the grain of wheat struggle up to meet the sun. (156)

Vanamee embodies a conscious awareness of his relationship and involvement with nature that is lacking in the other characters. Even the female characters, Hilma Tree and Annie Derrick, figure as symbolic embodiments of nature and do not contemplate or seem to be aware of the potential variations in the ways they might conceive the nonhuman world. Vanamee is alone in possessing this trait and thereby offers in the novel a solitary voice for the larger back-to-nature movement that was just gaining momentum in Norris's world.

Even as Vanamee lives close to nature, however, he lives in the human world too, participating in sheep herding and even plowing. While figuring in Norris's subplot of life and rebirth through his love of Angéle and her daughter, Vanamee also figures in a parallel subplot about the modern world of agriculture and nature. His role in modern agriculture is evident in one scene in which Vanamee climbs into the seat of a plow and participates in the massive "gang" plowing of the land:

> Perched on his seat, the moist, living reins slipping and tugging in his hands, Vanamee, in the midst of his steady confusion of constantly varying sensation, sight interrupted by sound, sound mingling with sight, on this swaying, vibrating seat, quivering with the prolonged thrill of the earth, lapsed to a sort of pleasing numbness . . . hypnotized by the weaving maze of things. (95)

This experience is not unpleasant for Vanamee. He is not only of nature; he is also of culture, participating in a massive human effort to transform the earth. The man of nature recognizes the place of agriculture in the larger order of the world. He is hardly repulsed by the sight of the long line of plows digging into the land; instead, he seems to enjoy a sexual energy from his agrarian labor. We follow the plows through the fields from Vanamee's point of view as he observes the spectacle of cultivation and sowing, "the long, stroking caress, vigorous, male, powerful, for which the earth seemed panting" (96). Vanamee has a corporeal dimension that understands and enjoys earthly pleasures; thus he understands his lusty coworkers who, following a day of labor, enjoy "a crude and primitive feasting" (97).

Vanamee is more than a shepherd and a plow man, however; he is also a mystic and visionary. While Presley, Annixter, Derrick, and Dyke inhabit a San Joaquin Valley dominated by vast agricultural fields and grassy foothills, Vanamee wanders in a world defined by strange and miraculous events that seem to defy nature as experienced by ordinary humans. On a moonlit summer night Vanamee wanders alone at the Seed ranch and is able, inexplicably, to perceive the colors of the flowers: "Pink became a royal red. Blue rose into purple. Yellow flamed into orange. Orange glowed golden and brilliant" (272). Ordinary men may not see colors under moonlight, but Vanamee not only sees them; he perceives them as intensified. Moreover, the Seed ranch, which had the previous fall occupied a small hollow near the Mission, has become a "little valley" large enough to hold a "million flowers—roses, lilies, hyacinths, carnations, violets" (274), flowers that in defiance of the seasons are all blooming at the same moment. It is a place that Norris describes in the same sentence as a "world of color" and a "darkness clogged and cloyed and thickened with sweet odors," defying all human sensory experience. It is not an actual place but one of the imagination—a place where one can see color in darkness, where roses and carnations, flowers that bloom in summer, are in full blossom with the hyacinths and lilies that bloom in early spring.[19]

Vanamee's presence in the novel is seemingly superfluous within the context of the larger narrative, but if we consider him within the context of the larger cultural movements with which Norris was familiar, the explanation of Vanamee's presence may be found. As Norris wrote *The Octopus*, nature writing was enjoying a rise in popularity in the nation. During the 1890s, while he lived and worked in the San Francisco Bay area, Norris's work appeared in such periodicals as the *Overland Monthly*, which also published the work of nature writers like John Muir and Mary Austin. Norris explicitly addresses nature writing in his 1903 essay, "The 'Nature' Revival in Literature," in which he describes the genre as "a return to the primitive, sane life of the country" (138).[20] It is unlikely that Norris consciously created Vanamee as a direct commentary on that movement; but it is possible that Norris, with his tendency for syncretism, created a character who embodied qualities that were floating about in the public discourse of his day. Vanamee may be an artifact, a reflection of Norris's peripatetic literary method, in which he haphazardly plucks ideas from movements without a larger mind to how they fit together. But Vanamee also bridges several of Norris's themes as he embodies a mystical connection to nature and a corporeal connection to the earth that is made through modern agricultural methods.

IN *THE OCTOPUS* Norris offers no coherent vision of the land; rather he suggests that it is always subject to perceptual systems, interpreted in varied ways that correspond to human goals. He suggests that California and the San Joaquin Valley are little more than the "scroll" on which he inscribes his epic. In committing this literary act, he effectively robs the land of its reality, attenuating it into an abstraction devoid of biological entities, both vegetative and animal; devoid of unique topographical features; and devoid of human communities who might have inhabited the land prior to the arrival of Magnus Derrick, Annixter, and Dyke. Norris reveals a rather insidious tendency in the ways he depicts the land on which he sets his story. It exists only as the arena where Anglo-European dramas are enacted, and its primary value is as the subject of language-mediated experience.

Norris reflects in *The Octopus* the tension apparent in Emerson that relates to questions of how one perceives the relationship among humans, their technologies, and their manipulations of the land and of how we might identify entities and behaviors that can be classified as "natural." Norris reveals that these categories become increasingly more difficult to differentiate as our manipulations of the land become entangled with technology and with our institutions. When he brings into his narrative the role of an amorphous yet compelling force driving all of creation, he suggests that ultimately all human activity is fundamentally natural. A paradox of Norris's vision, however, is that his characters seemingly reside at different nodes on a continuum that ranges from the extremely unnatural to the highly natural, with characters such as Derrick and Dyke occupying the unnatural end, mining the land without a sensitivity to the wider impacts of their behavior. At the end of the continuum closer to "natural" are such characters as Vanamee and the female characters Hilma and Annie Derrick. Vanamee, who promises to exist closest to nature, nonetheless engages in behaviors that embrace technology. Ultimately Norris defies a coherent reading as he explores the various limitations of the categories in which he had been steeped. The inconsistencies and paradoxes of *The Octopus* finally testify to the larger paradoxes surrounding human efforts to situate themselves in a larger cosmos that is simultaneously material and intellectual.

The Drama of

Reclamation

I N 1899 as Frank Norris was formulating his epic of wheat,
William Ellsworth Smythe was nearing completion of his own
nonfiction "epic," *The Conquest of Arid America*. Norris was
concerned with creating literature and conceived his work as a
fiction; Smythe was a reclamation booster who likely never shared
Norris's literary aspirations. If their two lives intersected, it was
through a shared familiarity with California and an awareness of
the larger political and social issues that were shaping agriculture.
Norris focused on the railroads as they affected agriculture; his
relative disinterest in irrigation is reflected in the lone irrigation
ditch that transected the Derrick ranch. Smythe's singular vision
was focused on water and the way it might be brought to the arid
lands of the American West, with the goal of creating farms for
the larger social good. Despite their contrasts, however, Norris and
Smythe share one compelling trait in the way they conceived of
the land: Norris abstracted the land in the interest of a higher
literary vision, and Smythe committed a similar act in the interest
of transforming public opinion.

Smythe, like Norris, was sensitive to the importance of region as
he situated himself in relation to his work. In the foreword to the
second edition of *The Conquest* (1905) Smythe reflects on the year

1899, when he was living "on a remote ranch in the desert country of Northeastern California, twelve miles from the nearest house" (ix).[1] This second edition of the book, he informs us, was completed in the library of his San Diego home, "with its seaward gable commanding a view of a populous town and wide landscape of bay, ocean, mountains, island, and the bold promontory of Point Loma" (ix). Region is also of vital importance to the irrigation movement, which began "remote from the great heart of the Nation" in the relatively unpopulated lands of the arid West. By 1905, he contends, the movement is now "planted in the heart of populous towns and intimately related to the commerce of the world" (ix).

In the foreword Smythe also tells another story that has far-reaching implications for his audience. Like Norris, Smythe writes at a desk, behind walls and windows, physically removed from the actual lands that are the subject of his writing. The visions and schemes he recounts are formed in the chambers of his imagination, and he seldom carries his ideas onto the actual land, into the environment to which they apply. Smythe gazes outward to an imagined natural scene and considers how the "peculiar environment of the arid region" (xi) exerts its influence on civilization. He seems not to recognize that the relationship might be considered in reverse, that he might examine how civilization exerts its influence on the environment.

Smythe writes the history of American expansion as a national drama whose final act will culminate in the massive irrigation of the American West. He defines history in terms of tropes, suggesting that we associate different phases of expansion with emblems: the *Mayflower*, which brought home-builders from Europe to New England, is the emblem for the first phase of history; the packhorse, which carried home-builders into the Kentucky wilderness and the Ohio Valley is the emblem for the second phase; and finally, the prairie schooner, which brought home-builders into the West, is the emblem of the third phase (18). *The Conquest* represents the culmination of Smythe's efforts to promote irrigation agriculture and the reclamation of desert lands, and it documents the role he played in the transformation of popular notions about the feasibility of farming in arid America.

Smythe was born in Massachusetts in 1861 to a family whose ancestors were early settlers of the region.[2] As a boy, he was inspired by the career of Horace Greeley, an influence that led him to take an apprenticeship in a printing office at age sixteen and to work for several New England papers. In 1888 Smythe moved to Nebraska, where he worked as a writer and editor for small newspapers. As a journalist he was in an ideal position to take up the banner for the irrigation crusade, when in 1890, Nebraska experienced a severe drought. There he observed men "shooting their horses and abandoning their farms" because of failed crops, while "several fine streams," which might figure as water sources for irrigation, flowed nearby. Smythe recalls: "There were the soil, the sunshine, and the waters, but the people did not understand the secret of prosperity, even with such broad hints before their eyes" (*CAA* 266).

Smythe had previously traveled to New Mexico and Colorado, where he had observed "thrifty orchards and gardens" that had been made possible by irrigation. He realized how Nebraska farmers could avoid future agricultural disasters if they employed similar irrigation systems. He therefore prevailed upon his editor at the *Omaha Bee*, Edward Rosewater, to allow him to write a series of articles on irrigation—a move that was not without risk of public backlash. Smythe recalls: "He gave me permission to do so on condition that I would sign the articles myself, as it was then considered little less than a libel to say that irrigation was needed in that part of the country" (266).

These articles commenced Smythe's career as a leading propagandist for the irrigation movement. He admits, "they changed my life completely. I had taken the cross of a new crusade"—a statement that suggests the religious underpinnings of his vision while possibly explaining the evangelical zeal with which he undertook his project of transforming "arid America" (266–67). Smythe not only promoted irrigation through his editorials; he began to stump for irrigation and helped to form the National

Irrigation Congress, which held its first convention in Salt Lake City in 1891. His wife, Harriett, describes Smythe as holding the "Chief responsibility for the executive conduct of the Irrigation Congress, first as secretary and later as chairman of its national committee" ("Biographical Sketch" 5).

Indeed, in the early years of the 1890s Smythe must have been a busy man. In addition to organizing and leading the National Irrigation Congress, he founded a journal, the *Irrigation Age*, which he edited until 1895. The *Irrigation Age* chronicled efforts to garner government support for irrigation, offered advice about irrigation farming, and promoted irrigation colonies by featuring glowing reports of their success. His work also found an audience in popular Eastern journals such as the *Atlantic Monthly*, *Century*, the *Review of Reviews*, *Forum*, and the *North American Review*. Many of the articles that appeared in these magazines were later included as chapters in *The Conquest of Arid America*.

As a writer, Smythe was a Johnny-one-note: throughout the 1890s he repeated a refrain that called for government support of reclamation, which would make possible the formation of irrigation colonies that would transform the West into a perfect agrarian society.[5] These colonies would be sustained by families practicing subsistence agriculture and would include good schools, ordered streets, and a thriving but wholesome social life. The philosophy expressed in *The Conquest* is one that Smythe had refined throughout the preceding decade.

In an editorial titled "The Republic of Irrigation" in the *Irrigation Age* Smythe describes the rising irrigated agrarian democracy that he and other irrigation proponents envision:

> The foundation of their philosophy of great average prosperity for common people will be the small farm, varying in different localities from ten acres to forty acres. Irrigation will make its crops absolutely sure and enable its proprietor to cultivate it intensely and scientifically to the end that each acre shall produce the largest possible crop of the best possible quality. (191)

A central component of his vision of a new agrarian democracy is the self-sufficient farm unit. He suggests that "each family shall produce, by a system of diversified farming, as nearly as possible everything it consumes" (191).

Smythe was impressed by Brigham Young's approach to community organization and farming, which centered in twenty-acre self-sustaining farms, and by Horace Greeley's Colorado colony, which was organized around eighty-acre parcels. Both colonies cultivated a range of diverse crops; farmers sold only what was not used by their own families as sustenance. Smythe believed that if farmers depended primarily on their solitary efforts for their livelihood, they removed themselves from the larger economic complex and thereby avoided the hardships associated with economic depressions. Patricia Limerick observes that in Smythe's vision, the farm would be "a bulwark against the tyranny of the surrounding social forces" (81). For Smythe, those tyrannical forces would be the same forces against which Populist farmers were rebelling. Although he never delivers an explicit Populist cry against the economic forces that were squeezing the farmers of the West, Smythe's remedy for farmers, subsistence rather than commercial agriculture, seems directed at eliminating their dependence on the very forces that the Populist movement was condemning.[4]

Smythe addressed the popular view of the desert and challenged common assumptions to persuade his audience to reenvision the arid West. Many of Smythe's contemporaries questioned that the dry lands could sustain large human populations and that irrigation was feasible or even desirable.[5] Their resistance to irrigation was inspired by a traditional view of the West as a parched wasteland—a view promulgated by early exploration narratives. Indeed, the list of stories of Western lands that describe the waterless and unpleasant conditions of the American West are varied and lengthy. The earliest accounts by such explorers as Lt. Zebulon M. Pike in 1810 and by Maj. Stephen H. Long in 1821 spoke of the region east of the Rocky Mountains as a barren desert (Opie 56). Martyn J. Bowden argues that this view of the "Great American Desert," which persisted until the middle of the century, was probably influenced most strongly by Major Long's accounts (51). As settlement in the plains regions progressed, accounts of the aridity of the Western lands became more highly differentiated. Notions of the great desert were gradually dispelled by such mid-century writers as Edwin Bryant, Virginia Reed Murphy, and Francis Parkman, whose narratives generally described a sparsely watered, but clearly not waterless, prairie. The most disturbing accounts of Bryant and Murphy dealt with the Great Basin, which was perhaps the most dauntingly arid territory in the West.

Edgar I. Stewart suggests that efforts to reshape public perceptions of the West began when land entrepreneurs sought to promote the sale of land and bonds. He describes how Jay Cooke and Company issued several pamphlets in the 1860s that frankly misrepresented conditions in the West. The region traversed by the Northern Pacific Railroad "was declared to have 'an adequate supply of atmospheric moisture for all purposes of agriculture and stock raising'" (26). The land was reported to be remarkably fertile and capable of sustaining profitable farming. William B. Hazen was among several who refuted these claims, however, arguing in an 1874 letter to the New York *Tribune* that the Northern Pacific Railroad was working "to make the world believe this section to be a valuable agricultural one" (cited in Stewart 35). Hazen, an army officer who had extensive experience in the Indian campaigns on the Great Plains, published a pamphlet entitled *Our Barren Lands* in 1875, which set out to refute the claims of land developers who sought to encourage settlement in the region west of the Mississippi.

By 1879, when John Wesley Powell published his survey of the lands of the American West, many were recognizing that the claims of promoters were blatantly false and that the prospects for agriculture in the arid West were not as promising as many would encourage land buyers to believe. In his *Report on the Lands of the Arid Region of the United States*, Powell addressed rainfall and water availability. He defined the "arid region" broadly as the area that "begins about midway in the Great Plains and extends across the Rocky Mountains to the Pacific Ocean" (11). His opening paragraph declares quite boldly that "the climate is so arid that agriculture is not successful without irrigation" (11)—a statement that was met with much hostility at the time but that would be recognized as accurate ten years later. In his survey Powell suggests that some regions of the arid lands would be appropriate for agriculture, but he describes the unequal rainfall throughout the West and the difficulties inherent in relying on that rain to support farming.

Fifteen years later, in 1894, Powell was still playing the devil's advocate in the water debates about the arid lands. In an article published in the *Irrigation Age* Powell argues that there are inherent limitations in the ability of the American people to develop and irrigate Western lands. Powell differs with Smythe and other reclamationists on two points: "The extent to which such agriculture can be carried on depends, first, upon the amount of water which a growing crop requires, and, second, upon the amount of water which can be artificially supplied" (54). In exploring the possibilities of capturing all runoff, he asserts, "It will never pay to impound the storm waters of sand deserts; it will never pay to impound the storm waters of bad lands; it will never pay to impound the storm waters of land of volcanic scoria; and there are many other minor conditions of storm-water catchment which are inhibitory" (62). Powell offers a voice of reason to reclamation boosters, pointing out the distinct features of the vast arid region that rendered visions of universal reclamation and water collection unreasonable. "Now it will never be practicable to catch all the water of maximum storms," he explains, "because of the great expense of constructing the necessary works" (62).

Powell argues that water is unevenly distributed through different regions and that the expense of capturing and delivering the water is prohibitive. Some districts enjoy a "large source of water supply, which is often limited only by the distance to which it can be practically carried by canals" (64). He also suggests that too much capital and labor has been expended, even in 1894, on ill-conceived irrigation projects, and he cautions that Smythe's vision of a fully developed West is unreasonable, observing that

"In no civilized country is all the land cultivated" (65). Powell advises the reclamationists:

> Before money or labor is to be invested in irrigating works, it becomes necessary to consider the water supply. Is there land? is the first question raised; Is there water? is the next question; and Can the water be carried to the land with reasonable economy is the third. Many canals have been constructed without a proper consideration of these three questions, and already capital has been wasted, and we have now reached a time in arid America when these three primary questions relating to irrigation enterprises should be properly answered, before lands are bought and sold, homes established, labor organized and capital invested. (65)

Powell's concerns, however, were generally dismissed. Even Smythe, who suggested in his editorial pages that a fair consideration of the irrigation issues included a discussion of the opposing views, devoted subsequent issues to articles refuting Powell's arguments.

Ultimately Powell's voice of temperance was silenced by the roar of entrepreneurial passion. Ironically Smythe included a lengthy acknowledgment of Powell in the second edition of *The Conquest*, applauding him as "a soldier, a poet, a scientist, a lover of his kind, but in no sense a man of practical commercial instincts" (261). Smythe commends Powell for conducting the first surveys of the West and suggests that he "saw the West with the eyes of a prophet and, with splendid imagination, beheld not only the opportunity which awaited a great people, but the measures which must be adopted to take best advantage of the opportunity" (262). Time transformed Powell into an ally in Smythe's crusade, while Powell's early and often negatively received advice was transformed into wisdom.

Powell offered scientific arguments for tempering the reclamation frenzy in 1894; other writers opposed irrigation on aesthetic or pseudoscientific grounds. In a book first published in 1901, *The*

Desert, John C. Van Dyke denounces plans to divert the Colorado River to irrigated farms: "Once in reservoirs it is to be distributed over the tract by irrigating ditches, and it is said a million acres of desert will thus be made arable, fitted for homesteads, ready for the settler who never remains settled" (57). Van Dyke seems almost to be speaking to Smythe, whose *The Conquest of Arid America* was published a year earlier. Van Dyke argues that while irrigated desert lands will certainly yield large crops, "the food that is produced there may prove expensive to people other than the producers" (58). He anticipates arguments that are later to prevail, that the real cost of irrigation is absorbed by taxpayers who support reclamation. Van Dyke's most significant opposition to irrigation, however, is unfounded. He objects to irrigation for the way it may alter climate, contending irrigation agriculture will increase desert humidity—"and that would be practically to nullify the finest air on the continent" (58). Perhaps Van Dyke's most eloquent argument against reclamation of the Colorado River basin is simply that some lands should not be altered by massive human intervention: "You cannot crop all creation with wheat and alfalfa. Some sections must lie fallow that other sections may produce. . . . The deserts should never be reclaimed. They are the breathing-spaces of the west and should be preserved forever" (59). Smythe seems largely untouched by these eloquent pleas for leaving some land uncultivated. He is the "practical man" whom Van Dyke denigrates, the man who sees the land only for its value in improving human society.

SMYTHE REVEALS that he is quite aware of the historical depiction of the West as a hostile territory when he observes that early accounts of the arid lands were "attended by many misrepresentations and strange misconceptions, which inevitably scattered wide the seeds of prejudice" (*CAA* 24). He is more immediately concerned, however, with the objections to reclamation and irrigation that were raised throughout the 1890s. *The Conquest of Arid America* is an implicit response to many of these objections, with Smythe presenting arguments that seem to offer overwhelming evidence that reclamation is desirable. Anticipating his readers' reservations, Smythe persuades them to adopt a new view of the desert and claims a position among a group of propagandists who, over the short course of a few decades, accomplished a transformation in notions about the feasibility of farming in arid America (Worster 67).

Smythe's crusade was initially inspired by his personal observations of the hardships faced by high plains farmers, but his call for reclamation was applied to diverse ecological regions of the arid West, from the Nebraska plains to the Great Basin, the Sonoran Desert of the Southwest, and the dry lands of California's Central Valley. Part of the charm of Smythe's plan was its very lack of specificity; it was applicable to arid lands everywhere. Homesteaders of the high plains region had been making efforts at farming for fifty years with varying degrees of success and failure that corresponded to rainfall cycles. A continuous wave of settlers—inspired by the notion of the "Manifest Destiny" of America's continued expansion westward to the Pacific—settled on the plains through the second half of the nineteenth century, only to have their farming efforts confounded by inadequate rainfall (Opie 63). Many learned dry-land farming techniques but found that these methods resulted in smaller crop yields than those enjoyed in more humid climates (63). Despite their own experience, Smythe observed, other farmers "clung stubbornly to the belief that, in some mysterious manner, rainfall increased with railroad building, settlement, and the cultivation of the land" (CAA 265).

Smythe recognized the drought of 1890 as an opportunity to reshape public opinion: "The psychological moment had come for the rise of a new cause which should take hold of the popular heart and go on, by a process of gradual unfoldment, until it became perhaps the greatest constructive moment of its time" (265). The following year Smythe carried his banner into a crowd that was on the cusp of accepting reclamation as a desirable means of resolving their own persistent problems with drought. His approach to establishing a new public regard for irrigation, and of legitimizing reclamation, was to develop an argument for developing the West that was embedded in a larger narrative history of the American people.

Smythe begins his argument for reclamation by developing a history of the United States, which he defines in terms of tropes. Like Crèvecoeur, who described American expansion as a series of successions, Smythe suggests that we interpret the history of westward settlement in phases.[6] Moreover, Smythe casts history as a drama, focusing on isolated moments as a means of establishing a plot that corresponds to the three acts. The history of the United States is a cavalcade: "The first act in the drama of American settlement ended in the eastern foothills of the Alleghany mountains about 1770; the second, in the neighborhood of the Mississippi River about 1860, the third, midway on the plains of Dakota, Nebraska, Kansas, and Texas, about 1890." In his final paragraph he tells us: "The wonderful drama of American colonization has reserved a fourth and crowning act, for which the scenery is arranged and the actors ready" (18).

Smythe's assertion that history is a drama unfolding in acts on an environmental stage carries with it some rather disturbing implications. In casting Euro-American progress as a play, he perceptually transforms the very real land into a set on which events are played out. This abstracting of the land, which is similar to Norris's fictional abstracting, has the effect of stripping the environment of its actuality. The land loses its distinguishing features as its previous human and nonhuman inhabitants are erased from the scene. In calling for a reenvisioning of the desert, Smythe draws on the theatrical trope to assist his audience to reinterpret their perceptions of the land and to reconsider the elements of the land as merely components of a scene that can be manipulated, shifted about, and reconfigured to result in a new scene.

By setting history within the context of a theatrical production in which the land figures as the stage, Smythe engages in a remarkably literary act, one that now resounds as remarkably postmodern in his suggestion that "reality" is defined by the language—the tropes and metaphors—employed in its description. By describing the desert as a dramatic scene, the force of the actual activities he proposes—that is, reconstructing the desert land—is attenuated into an abstraction. Smythe neglects to describe the great earthmovers and cranes, the train cars of gravel, concrete, and steel carried into river canyons, and the tons of dynamite that will blast tunnels to divert river flows. He offers no image of the backstage process necessary to realize his vision; instead, he presents a dramatic production that will convince through its appeal to emotions and thereby transform perceptions of the arid lands.

Smythe's version of United States history affirms the popular ideology of the day: America is a great nation. His history begins not with Jamestown or Plymouth but with "the surrender of Cornwallis at Yorktown" (3).[7] As a rhetorical move, Smythe establishes the strategy he will follow throughout *The Conquest of Arid America*: he selects a concept that his audience will accept as a widely held truth, challenges it, and replaces it with a new truth— which in this case is that American history doesn't begin in 1607 or in 1620 but in 1781, the moment when Anglo-Americans turned their sights from Europe and the past to the West and the future of America. He next suggests that until 1781 Americans were "merely European sentinels standing guard over a treasure of continental magnitude, which they neither comprehended nor appreciated" (3)—an observation few would have disputed. In this way Smythe gently reshapes a perception of history, subtly rewriting some elements while retaining others to suggest a tradition with which all Americans are familiar. Smythe invokes few specific examples of history; instead, he falls back on the stock phrases of American progressive boosterism. This tactic has a curious affect: Smythe subtly cloaks the implicit argument he develops by embedding it in a narration, an American cavalcade of progress that carries us from the steamboat to the iron horse. The result is that readers, fired by the passion of the story, participate in the fiction while missing the fact that these misrepresentations of reality are actually the premises of his argument. Thus Smythe creates an implied argument that will appear sound as long as these questionable premises remain unexamined.

In writing this history, Smythe commits a literary act that

has curious textual and socioenvironmental implications. On one hand, he sets out to write a book documenting the history of reclamation—an account he claims is founded on fact. He presents his "history" as an accurate rendering of events, yet on the other hand, at various points he acknowledges the storytelling dimension of his work. In a chapter he added to the second edition, "The Rise of a New Cause," Smythe opens his discussion by asserting:

> The true history of irrigation in America would involve a comprehensive study of the life of the Western people during the past two generations, with a study of certain communities which trace their civilization to a period much more remote. The facts for such a history would be found in the record of exploration and colonization. (CAA 261)

Smythe writes in a conditional mood, reflecting on what might figure as a true history, and suggests in succeeding sentences that he is purposefully ignoring these dimensions to consider only one part of that history: "the subject will be sketched in relation to one aspect only" (261).

He acknowledges the problems inherent in creating a history and in accomplishing the necessary task of including certain pieces of information while excluding others. Smythe seems to be providing us with certain clues about his own narrative project, as if to provide us with subtextual reasons for disregarding his authority. To follow *The Conquest of Arid America* in the sequence Smythe creates is to follow a convoluted and confounded tale. It is a strange patchwork of articles pieced together from other publications and chapters added in the second edition. Indeed, it seems quite odd that Smythe pauses to reflect on the nature of his narrative task rather late in the second edition, on page 261 of a 349-page book. He invites us, in effect, to reconsider how he develops his history of the West and the American people and encourages us to look for other counternarratives that might be embedded in his story.[8]

In writing history as a dramatic cavalcade involving Puritans and pioneers, Smythe asserts that American history is the chronicle of the Anglo-Saxon Americans to whom he directs his book. In the introduction to the first edition of *The Conquest* (1900), he condemns the imperialist tendencies that carry Americans to "the tropical islands of the Pacific and Caribbean," and he suggests that the "true mission" of Americans is "not to impose their dominion upon distant lands and alien peoples, but to work out the highest forms of civilization for their own race and nationality" (xiii). This seemingly anti-imperialist assertion has its dark side. Smythe's objections to American expansion into distant lands is based on his belief that the western United States still holds room for a hundred million people. For Smythe, social and environmental domination are conflated. The land upon which Smythe forms his vision is curiously vacant of earlier occupants. Native Americans and Mexicans are entirely absent, having been relegated to a vague and distant past even though they are still inhabitants of the land. African Americans are completely overlooked. Throughout *The Conquest* Smythe refers to Anglo-Saxons as the dominant race, whom he defines not in opposition to the native peoples but to the European immigrants who were spilling into the cities of the American East.[9]

Smythe's social vision is designed for white Americans, whose middle-class existence is being threatened by the growing population of the eastern United States, who are competing for jobs, land, and social influence. His uneasiness about the expanding immigrant population is suggested in the first edition when he explains, "We shall consider how surplus men and money may be brought to surplus resources, and applied, under sound business principles, to the making of homes, industries, and institutions *in consonance with the traditions of our race and the genius of our people*" (xv; italics mine). Elements of social and environmental domination converge as Smythe hints at Anglo-Saxon separatism defined by region. The social elevation of white Americans will be made possible through their environmental mastery of a new land. His scheme is to create homes for middle-class Americans while leaving the masses of immigrants to their messy lot in the congested cities of eastern America. The pristine and undeveloped lands of the American West will provide the ground where Anglo-Saxon Americans may enact and fulfill their Manifest Destiny.

Smythe's rationale for opening his book on reclamation with a refocusing of American history becomes clear when we consider the racial undercurrent in his work. In his first chapter Smythe establishes that the American people are industrious and that their land is remarkably rich with resources necessary to build a great nation. He exalts the imperialist tendencies of Euro-Americans while simultaneously implying their deficiencies by arguing for the potential of the United States to be an even greater nation than it is now. Continuing his revision in the next chapter, "The Home-Building Instinct of the American People," Smythe shifts his focus from the material wealth of the nation to the apparently innocent motives underlying American expansion, which were rooted in an instinct to create homes. He explains that the Western explorer and settler wanted only "to live there at peace with his neighbors and the world, to make better institutions for average humanity—this . . . is seen to have been the consistent aim of American colonization from the beginning" (12–13). This statement seems to challenge all known information about the relationship between Native Americans and white American settlers. As he completed the first edition of his book, Smythe was living in northern California, where white settlers were actively engaging in genocide and the displacement of the local native inhabitants. Smythe acknowledges the rapacious motives of the gold-seekers of California but dismisses them as an aberration. That he so readily overlooks the violation of native peoples living in the lands occupied by Anglo-Americans may indicate that this native population is conflated with the land itself in his scheme and is, in effect, invisible.

Smythe implies that the Americans whom he addresses trace their family histories in the United States to earlier centuries. The "home-building instinct" began with the "Puritan in Massachusetts, the Baptist in Rhode Island, the Quaker in Pennsylvania, and the Catholic in Maryland," who were more concerned with "the babies in their cradles" than with "their spires and crosses" (14). The next "real era of colonization" occurred after the American Revolution. Smythe describes how the population of the Ohio and Mississippi Valleys grew between 1790 and 1820, yet he does not suggest that this population might have been bolstered by immigrants; rather, he presents this phase of growth as an extension of the previous phase, thereby suggesting that it was a continuous internal increase in population by Americans reproducing from one generation to the next.

Smythe accomplishes his exclusion of new arrivals without explicit comment by directing his words to "the great middle-classes." That this middle class is already privileged is suggested when he observes that "only three per cent. of our people travel more than fifty miles from their homes in the course of a year. Those who make extended pleasure tours gravitate not unnaturally to Europe" (20). The unfortunate effect of this, according to Smythe, is that they are ignorant of the West and "the true significance of the wide empire" it represents—a significance that exists in its economic potential for the middle classes living amidst the "idle and burdensome . . . surplus population" of the East (19). Obviously Smythe is distinguishing his audience from another body of people, whom we might guess to be the recent arrivals to the American scene.

SMYTHE'S TASK of rewriting United States history is only one part of his larger rhetorical effort. In suggesting that history is an incomplete drama, he implies that the drama must move toward a conclusion. Smythe also challenges objections to reclamation to convince his audience that the arid lands offer the space and provide the setting wherein the American dream can be enacted. To do this, however, Smythe must first convince his audience that the desert is indeed not the wasteland depicted by many.

Smythe begins his implicit rebuttal to anticipated objections to his vision by proposing that the arid lands have been misunderstood by American farmers, who are unable to identify truly fertile lands. Anticipating a common objection to the relatively treeless lands of the West, Smythe speaks to early plains settlers who believed that "no soil was fit for agricultural purposes unless it furnished the pioneer an opportunity to cut down trees and pull up stumps" (20).[10] He challenges the notion that a land that will not sustain trees will not support agriculture, and he even introduces an undercurrent of ridicule in his assessment of the settlers' ignorance:

> "Land that won't grow trees won't grow anything," was the maxim of the knowing ones. Their fathers had cleared the forests on the slopes of the Alleghanies to make way for the plough and the field, and the new generation could not conceive that land which bore rich crops of wild grasses and lay plastic and level for the husbandman to begin his labors could have any value. (20)

According to Smythe, American farmers wasted considerable time clearing a land of its trees, when they could have looked to the "land beyond the Mississippi." When they eventually did look to treeless land, they discovered "new and superior conditions" (20), including a territory that did not require clearing.

In developing his extended literary metaphor, Smythe suggests a semiological misreading of the land:

> One must live in the Far West to begin to comprehend it. Not only so, but he must come with eager eyes from an older civilization, and he must study the beginnings of industrial and social institutions throughout the region as a whole, to have any adequate appreciation of the real potentialities of that half of the United States which has been reserved for the theatre of twentieth-century developments. To all other observers the new West is a *sealed book*. (21; italics mine)

Thus Smythe informs us that the land has been misinterpreted by readers looking for the wrong signs. Farmers have been applying old knowledge to new conditions. In looking to trees as evidence of arability, they have overlooked the incipient fertility of arid soils. By regarding the features of the land as signs, Smythe abstracts those features, suggesting not that they are a part of a vital and interactive natural system but that they are merely symbols on a theatrical stage that might be interpreted in a variety of ways—as impediments to cultivation or as signs of fertility, for instance.

Smythe refutes arguments against the arability of Western lands by inverting generally accepted conceptions about arid regions. Rather than defend the desert, he first attacks conceptions of farming in more humid climates. Such farming, he argues, is "childlike" because the farmers are depending on "the mood of the clouds" (21–22) to water their crops. Smythe denigrates humid climates and then promotes the superiority of arid lands by identifying them as the ideal setting for science-based agriculture. In humid lands, farmers must contend with rain, which randomly deposits water across the land in unmeasured amounts. Perverse nature will "rain alike . . . on the strawberries, which would be benefited by it, and on the sugar-beets, which crave only the uninterrupted sunshine" (47). The arid lands offer a special opportunity for farmers, who will realize a control over nature that is lacking elsewhere. Reclamation will provide the means of control, and the farmer will be able to determine, independent of the larger climate, how much water is deposited on a crop, a field, and even an entire region.

Smythe expands on the notion that arid lands have been misunderstood. Not only has their agricultural potential been misinterpreted; their potential for shaping people and their institutions has been ignored. Smythe unfolds this portion of his argument in several parts to demonstrate how the desert is a place where people might best understand their relationship with nature. He first invokes the rhetoric of the nascent tourist industry of the Southwest and considers the climate of the arid regions, which many were beginning to recognize as particularly beneficial for such conditions as tuberculosis and arthritis. Smythe addresses popular objections that irrigation agriculture would result in health problems for those living in its midst. The arid lands offer salutary benefits while providing a more amiable climate. He cites scientific evidence that dry heat and cold are far more tolerable than their humid counterparts, describing how the United States Weather Service measures relative humidity; we are assured that "a cold of thirty degrees below zero at Helena, in Montana, is felt less than ten degrees above zero in Chicago or New York" (25) and that the "dryness, purity, and lightness of the atmosphere" contribute to a healthy environment because it "neither breeds diseases nor carries their germs" (26). The conclusion Smythe draws from his observations is that in addition to being the "nation's treasure-house," the desert is "the nation's sanitarium" (27).

Drawing on the work of pioneering soil scientist Eugene W. Hilgard, Smythe suggests that arid lands figured as the centers of early Western civilization because of their "phenomenal fertility" (34). Smythe correctly surmises that ancient civilizations arose in fertile regions that enjoyed abundant water supplies. He does not pause to question why those civilizations later declined—a fact that, as many have come to understand, was the result of decreased soil fertility and diminished crop production, complicated by soil salinization caused by irrigation itself.[11] He focuses instead on the magnificence of those cultures in their most highly evolved and bureaucratic eras—to imply that the American West could also realize the glories of a Mesopotamia or an Egypt.

For Smythe, however, the most important trait of arid land is that it defines and shapes the institutions, the customs, and the individual habits of the people who occupy the region. When taken at face value, this idea might be compatible with such modern environmentalist notions as bioregionalism. However, for Smythe, the way that natural conditions shape human institutions is somewhat novel: adaptation means that Americans must work cooperatively, rather than individually, to overcome nature. The historical problem with humid lands, he argues, is that water has been abundant and that farmers could therefore establish their homesteads without any need for communal cooperation. The fact that they could locate their farms and homes wherever they pleased resulted in land greed and in extremely large farms, a situation that in turn resulted in their isolation. In other words, Smythe argues that humid climates have encouraged social isolation, greed, competition, and finally, monopolies by allowing people to settle and establish their homesteads wherever they pleased. But, fortunately, arid lands demand "associative enterprise" (32), which will obviate all of these problems by requiring that settlers organize themselves around central irrigation bureaucracies that will democratically distribute the collected water.

IN THE SECOND edition of *The Conquest of Arid America* Smythe includes a chapter that introduces a spiritual dimension to his argument, which is lacking in the first edition. In "Man's Partnership with God" Smythe seems to respond to writers such as John C. Van Dyke and Mary Austin, who popularized the notion that the desert is a land to be valued for its beauty and spiritual possibilities.[12] Smythe asserts in his closing argument that the arid lands represent an ideal spiritual realm as a God-given land. The larger message of his book might be summarized in a paragraph:

> The waste of the desert and mountain has been unsympathetically called "the land that God forgot." Time will show, and already time has begun to show, that above all other sections Arid America is the God-remembered land. He evidently remembered that somewhere there must be a place where man should become supremely alive to his divinity—that somewhere he must be driven by the club of necessity into a brotherhood of labor—that somewhere the material must be blended with the spiritual until man should stand erect, the conscious partnership of the universe. (327–28)

Smythe's vision for America resonates with the Old Testament. In discovering God's ways, the children of Israel will realize their destiny in the new Eden of the American West. The land is incomplete and waits for mankind to bring their God-given talents and water to a rich soil. Divinity is found in partnership with nature in the desert, through which humans will realize a partnership with God. In this conclusion Smythe suggests that men must work "in harmony with the universe," and he reinforces this theme by urging his readers that humans must "adapt themselves" (329) to the new conditions of the arid lands. He argues that the political structures in place to govern a nation must speak to the lands that fall under its control. Just as nature governs the land, "The same influence is dominant in the formation of institutions. Laws and customs must conform to environment, and to the work to be done under the conditions which environment imposes" (329–30). The unsympathetic desert offers the opportunity for men to unite to know their environment and, by extension, God's ways.

In considering Smythe's ideas, one might readily identify the extent to which notions of environmental harmony and adaptation have evolved in the past century. There is something gravely amiss in Smythe's notion of adaptation or conformity. For him, adaptation means that humans use "scientific knowledge" to understand desert conditions and ultimately transform arid land into arable land. When Smythe suggests that institutions adapt "in conformity with the ascertained facts" (330), he is arguing that government should provide the means to apply scientific knowledge to the project of reconfiguring the land for farming. This, for him, represents institutional response to the environment. Human adaptation means not a scaling-down of agricultural expectations but a scaling-up of human effort. He reaches this conclusion through a convoluted argument, submerged in a larger tale about American destiny that leads his readers to an undeniable conclusion: irrigation of the American West is consistent with divine providence and is, therefore, good.

Smythe's plan for the West is certainly not intended as a panacea for the problems of all Americans; rather, it is intended for those whom he describes as a "certain class of settlers" (303)—namely, Anglo-Americans who possess enough capital to relocate from the congested East and begin a new enterprise in the West. In his second edition of *The Conquest* Smythe includes a chapter entitled "Preparing Homes for the People." This chapter warns that ideal farm colonies are not available to everyone and cautions that the settler of arid America must possess enough capital "to bring his farm to a paying stage" (303), a requisite that essentially excludes the poor laborers of Eastern cities. In addition to speaking to Smythe's vision of the West as a refuge for the middle class, this allusion to initial capital investments provides a subtextual hint at the way that commercial interests were dominating Western land-development schemes. He tells us: "It is important that the reader should understand at the outset that a large part of the land to be reclaimed by the national irrigation system is not public domain, open to entry under the land laws, but land in private ownership which the settler may only obtain by purchase from its present proprietors" (303). While Smythe hopes for a socioenvironmental Eden for the honest Anglo-Saxon Americans, his language cannot veil the fundamental paradox of his scheme, which encourages entrepreneurism while expecting that humans will transcend the profit motive.

Smythe's vision for humanity is rather naive. His drama for the American West apparently has a cast of characters who undergo modifications in human nature. In the fourth act, which will unfold over the twentieth century, Smythe anticipates that humans will shed the cupidity that has afflicted them in earlier acts. Perhaps Smythe cannot conceive of the irrigation empire that will later rise in the American West, and when he promotes his vision, he is not conceiving of a Las Vegas, a Phoenix, or a Los Angeles. Neither is he considering the greed of the individual small farmer. His model farmer embodies Jeffersonian values and seems interested only in eking out a modest living for himself and his family. Indeed, Smythe reserves all greedy motives for unspecified capitalists and industrialists, and he seems largely unaware that Americans have a lengthy tradition of land hunger and of claiming and farming tracts that are far larger than can be efficiently managed by a single family.[13] He acknowledges the "armed conquests for spoils, and power, and martial glory" among Europeans and Asians, but he suggests that "It was far different with the men who, at various periods during the last three hundred years, conquered the soil of the United States and extended the frontiers of its civilization" (13).

Although Smythe seems to promote his vision with a blind imperialistic zeal, his concern for the lot of the average middle-class white man and woman appears to be sincere. He dreams of a Jeffersonian democracy—ideal communities of neatly tended gardens, tidy houses, and well-organized schools that will rear upstanding citizens who will steer arid America toward an ever-more idyllic future. In addition, Smythe's vision speaks to the condition of farm women. Like many of his peers advocating cooperative farm colonies, Smythe is sensitive to the way that the pioneering spirit of Westward-reaching men affects the women who follow them in their ventures. In his introduction, he advises the married men who are contemplating relocation from the East to the West to consider their wives. He suggests that the excitement and the vision of reshaping a new land may not be "shared by the average woman," who is more sensitive to her surroundings and might be unhappy with austere landscapes of the American West. He likely comes closest to recognizing the true hardships endured by pioneer women when he states, "Or it may be—and this is more likely—that she gets the heavier end of the burdens peculiar to the pioneer" (xx). Smythe points to the situation of farm women also identified by Hamlin Garland and Liberty Hyde Bailey: women isolated on farms are deprived of human contact as they face mean working conditions.[14] Smythe acknowledges that women have been hardest hit by the pioneering instinct of American men, and he suggests that farm colonies will help to obviate much of the social isolation that makes American farm life unpleasant for women. Because farming will be conducted at a subsistence level rather than for commercial gain, the farmers will not be entangled in the market forces that make agriculture so troublesome and unsatisfying; their lives and work will be focused on sustaining their families.

IN THE *Conquest of Arid America* Smythe examines land that his peers would regard as "wasteland" and argues that this territory is highly desirable, worthy of not just attention but also settlement. He tells his readership that they have been sorely mistaken in their assessment of aridity as a curse and a limitation to farming. The arid lands are especially meaningful because they demand that people come together, working not as solitary individuals but as communities. The desert lands offer a ground where mankind can come into awareness of "his divinity" through attending to the limitations of the land. Smythe suggests that God has intentionally left the desert unfinished: "nature neglects to water it with unfailing rains" as a lesson to men, who must learn "a better way to pray" (*CAA* 328). The prayers of the modern farmer bring a scientific inspiration rather than rain: the understanding that irrigation is the technique by which the desert will be conquered.[15]

Smythe might be yet another minor player in Western environmental history were it not for the way he helped to facilitate a shift in public perceptions that made possible the development of reclamation projects throughout the West in the twentieth century. Donald Worster has suggested that Smythe helped to legitimize irrigation and reclamation for an American public who were skeptical about its value. "Legitimation," Worster explains, "involves the transforming of what might be regarded with skepticism or hostility into something acceptable, even honorific" (*Rivers of Empire* 114). Other historians, such as Donald Pisani, have shared Worster's view that wide popular support for the development of the twentieth-century water projects could occur "only after certain assumptions and stereotypes about the West were challenged" (70). Such a shift in public perceptions, labeled by Worster as "legitimation," might also be seen as a revision in what environmentalists variously refer to as a "worldview" or a "paradigm."[16] Fritjof Capra has described a social paradigm as "a constellation of concepts, values, perceptions, and practices shared by a community, which form a particular vision of reality that is the basis of the way the community organizes itself" ("Systems Theory" 335). A paradigm shift occurs when "that particular vision of reality" is transformed. Among environmentalists the term "paradigm shift" is generally reserved to describe the recent heightened environmental consciousness of the past few decades, which is characterized by an ecocentric rather than an anthropocentric experience of nature. Given this definition, one might ironically interpret Smythe's *The Conquest of Arid America* as an effort to create such a shift in concepts, values, and perceptions to allow for the creation of federally supported irrigation projects in the American Southwest.[17]

Smythe's efforts at transforming public perceptions, obviously, emerge from an impulse quite different from modern followers of deep ecology and from followers of what Michael Zimmerman calls the "New Paradigm."[18] These philosophic camps propose that we face a global environmental crisis that will be mitigated only when humans undergo a personal transformation in their perceptions of nature. Rather than perceiving themselves as dominant over nature, they would regard themselves as yet another element within a larger network of creation. Smythe also calls for a shift in human perceptions about the environment to facilitate our new relationship with it, but his call for transformation in perceptions is directed not at minimizing our interactions with nature but at maximizing our awareness of how we can dominate nature.

This domination, however, has some rather strange resonances with the modern prescriptions for resolving environmental problems. Smythe envisions new possibilities for the land—ones that many of his peers found laughable—when he calls for communities of small farmers who would engage in subsistence-level agriculture. He rails against what he calls in a section heading the "ONE CROP ERROR IN THE WEST" (*RI* 191), which is motivated by a desire for quick profit. Smythe cites an unidentified "resident of the San Joaquin valley of California" who points out that those who work in the arid region generally practice a profligate management of its resources:

> We let our timber rot and buy fencing. We throw away our ashes and grease and buy soap. We raise dogs and buy hogs. We let our manure go to waste and buy guano. We grow weeds, and buy vegetables and brooms. We catch five-cent fish with a four-

dollar rod. We build school houses and send our children off to be educated. And, lastly, we send our boys out with a forty-dollar gun and a ten-dollar dog to hunt for ten-cent birds. (*RI* 191)

Smythe seems to criticize a modern consumerism that encourages the purchase of goods that might be produced at home from the resources at hand. He advocates a subsistence lifestyle as a way of ensuring the well-being of individuals and families and, most importantly, their communities. He argues against single-crop agriculture not because such farming encourages a loss of biological diversity but because such a practice forces farm families to rely on the larger economy to meet their basic living needs. Moreover, single-crop agriculture traditionally had been practiced by farmers such as those depicted by Norris—farmers motivated by profit who exhausted the fertility of the soil by growing the same crop year after year and then abandoned the land and moved on to more fertile ground, where they would repeat the process. For Smythe the sin of one-crop agriculture is that it is market-oriented and not family-oriented.

The rationale for Smythe's positions differs considerably from that of modern environmentalists. He argues for reshaping perceptions of the land and for practicing a diverse subsistence-level agriculture as a solution to problems in human society. If the land itself benefits from a more economical subsistence-approach to farming, this is merely incidental to the benefit to the people living on that land. Modern agrarian environmentalists have introduced an ecological dimension to arguments for subsistence agriculture, suggesting that small-scale family farms will benefit not just the families and, by extension, their communities but that such farms will result in a better care of the land.[19]

Smythe's proposals now seem oddly eccentric when we consider that he never addresses the "backstage" elements of his schemes. Even when one considers the seemingly altruistic intentions behind his vision, it is nonetheless difficult for any reader of the late twentieth century to overlook the obvious problems with *The Conquest of Arid America*. In setting his discussion within the context of a stage, Smythe encourages us to overlook all that might be behind that stage. His drama is enacted on an arid land, which, he implies, nonetheless enjoys an unlimited water supply. His argument focuses on the stage itself, which are the blooming desert lands, and the players, which are the thriving communities of conscientious citizens and their healthy, vital children. Questions about adequate rainfall that will fill the rivers, the massive effort that must figure in reserving that water, or the long-term consequences do not enter into his scheme. By writing United States history and destiny as a drama, Smythe compels the audience to trust that water will be delivered, perhaps via a deus ex machina such as the federal government.

Smythe sidesteps scientifically based objections like those posed by Powell, which address the overall adequacy of the supply of Western water, reclaimed or unreclaimed, to support the kind of agriculture Smythe proposes. Smythe implies that desert farmers will enjoy an unlimited supply of reserved water upon which they can draw for irrigation and that farmers of arid lands will not have to worry about a capricious nature that may impose periods of drought or deluge. He simply ignores the logical questions posed by skeptics. Such a tactic seems reasonable within the scope of a narrative history or a drama or in a cavalcade intended to fire the passion of its audience; thus Smythe can run loose with his assertions, having prepared his audience to become caught up in the drama of his story. Smythe appears to be less interested in creating the conditions necessary to bring his drama to a conclusion than in garnering support for his cause.

Smythe's vision of a massively reclaimed West has come to pass through a collective public agreement to overcome rather than adapt to the natural conditions of the land at any cost, either economic or environmental. This public consensus has been realized through a perpetuation of Smythe's strategy of ignoring the "backstage" considerations. Patricia Limerick has observed that Smythe makes the actual desert lands seem "oddly irrelevant" (88). Indeed, in formulating his plan for the people, he fails to consider the life of the desert itself and the environmental consequences of reclamation—a failure that his rhetorical approach itself may have created and encouraged: in envisioning history and American "destiny" as a drama, he extracts it from the actual social, political, and physical realities of his world. He simplifies reclamation for his readers by transforming it into an enterprise occurring on an abstracted landscape, unpopulated by real people, plants, or animals. This simplification also likely contributed to his success. While his historical drama, which culminates in a society of small farms, is doomed to exist forever in the realm of fiction, his dramatic trope did help to transform popular opinion about the feasibility of reclamation and irrigation agriculture.

Smythe's legacy is that he helped to found a hydraulic empire. He and his fellow advocates of reclamation were able to accomplish their shift in public perception relatively quickly because they drew on traditional views of United States history and wrote reclamation as a continuation of a tradition. In *The Conquest of Arid America* Smythe invokes widely accepted so-called truths and gently reshapes them to suggest that the dream of reclamation is consistent with American values. As I consider how the fourth act of his drama has played out, however, I believe he might best be remembered not for his ill-conceived vision of small farm communities but for the way his efforts contributed to a shift in public perception that facilitated the transformation of the desert he knew into a land he probably never could have imagined.

The Conquest of Arid America is a nonfiction text that reveals values evident in the work of both Frank Norris and Hamlin Garland. Like Garland, Smythe embraced a faith in the small farm and hoped to see its revival and endurance in the American West. There, however, their similarities begin and end. Smythe embraced agriculture and environmental transformation as he disregarded the nonhuman nature that characterized the lands he hoped to transform. While Garland suggested that farmers might better grapple with nature if they could overcome the economic obstacles to their success, Smythe asserted that the mastering of nature through irrigation would itself allow the farmer to overcome these obstacles.

Nature, Science,

and Agriculture

O F THE writers I consider here, Liberty Hyde Bailey Jr. (1858–1954) addresses most directly the complex relationship among the individual, society, and the environment. Bailey's interest in farming is implicit throughout his work. He regards agriculture as part of a larger social and biological order; thus he does not bring the focused attention to farm life that Garland brought to his stories in *Main-Travelled Roads* or that Norris brought to *The Octopus*. Unlike Smythe, who concentrated his energy on the cause of irrigation, Bailey quietly devoted his life to the horticulture that figured in successful agriculture. His interest in the larger social and biological questions surrounding farm life resulted from an awareness that agriculture exists at the nexus of nature and culture.

Among the writers I have addressed, Bailey is the only scientist. He recognized that human perception, like that of all animals, is necessarily species-centered, but he also was aware that we humans are unique among animals through the magnitude of the transformations we bring to our habitats. Moreover, Bailey balanced his objective scientific sensibility with a spirituality that acknowledged an intangible and unmeasurable dimension of human existence. Bailey might be regarded as an early environmentalist for his belief that our "dominion" over the planet must be balanced with a sense of responsibility toward the natural entities we transform. His particular philosophical perspective on the relationship between humans and the environment might best be described as enlightened anthropocentrism. Bailey advocated a wide public understanding and appreciation for nonhuman nature and believed that an understanding of the plants, animals, and other entities that define our world will enrich us both individually and collectively as a society. Unlike many of his peers in the early years of this century, who were taking up the call of nature appreciation through wilderness study and the "woodcraft" and back-to-the-land movements, Bailey encouraged his readers to discover the realm of a possibly more mundane nonhuman nature surrounding us in our daily lives in our dooryards, neighborhoods, and farms.

Bailey, like William Smythe, esteemed the family farm as a cornerstone of democracy, and like Emerson and Garland, he recognized the farm as a place where a spiritual connection to the earth might be realized. Historians have dismissed Smythe's vision surrounding the small farm for its grandiosity. Bailey's has suffered a similar fate, his views of farming having been dismissed as nostalgic and sentimental.[1] Indeed, Bailey's work can sometimes exhibit both these qualities, but his nostalgia for his childhood way of life should not diminish the strength and the vision of his message. He argued for preserving the family farm, in part, because of his own positive associations with farms. But like many modern advocates of sustainable agriculture, he argued for preserving small farms because he observed that farmers employ techniques that conserve, rather than destroy, an agricultural land when their interest in that land is vested in ownership and inheritance.[2] Moreover, Bailey believed that a spiritual experience of nature was not lost in farming, and he believed that this spiritual dimension should be acknowledged when one is considering agriculture scientifically. Bailey sought to promote a wider understanding of the personal rewards that could be found in farming, yet he also was a horticulturist who understood the economic aspects of agriculture and its status as a business implicated in, and dependent upon, the sciences.

Liberty Bailey's life spanned almost a century. Born in Michigan in 1858, he spent his childhood on the family farm at South Haven, on the eastern shore of Lake Michigan.[3] Bailey's father had purchased the land in 1845, when the region was still regarded as a wilderness where an enterprising man might establish himself and his family. He diligently labored at clearing his property of native trees and eventually planted an apple orchard, one that would become "one of the most noted in Michigan's pomological history" (Rodgers 7). Over the years, he expanded his farm, planting another orchard and, as his three sons matured, involving them in the cultivation and upkeep of the trees that were the family's livelihood. Liberty Bailey Jr., the youngest of the sons, took a great interest in not only the family orchard but also the family garden. He demonstrated an aptitude for natural history in his explorations of the countryside surrounding his home, often collecting local plants and small animals to study in his spare time. His family and teachers nurtured this interest, and with their encouragement, young Bailey expanded his knowledge through both observation and formal study. Although books were carefully guarded and sometimes scarce in rural Michigan, Liberty Bailey managed to locate ones that inspired his imagination, including Charles Darwin's *On the Origin of Species by Means of Natural Selection*, and Asa Gray's *Field, Forest and Garden Botany*.

Liberty Bailey was a promising student and a budding leader. Recognizing his special talents, Bailey's mother rallied the support of Liberty Sr., and together, they encouraged their son to attend the Michigan Agricultural College, the land-grant college that would later become Michigan State University. From 1877 to 1882, when he was a student there, Bailey's natural leadership blossomed. He was instrumental in establishing the campus newspaper, the *Speculum*, and his work on the paper marked the beginning of his career as a writer. Bailey was twenty-five years old when graduated from the college.

Following his graduation, Bailey worked briefly as a reporter for the *Springfield (Illinois) Morning Monitor*. Early in 1883 his career took a sharp turn in a new direction when he became the assistant to the Harvard botanist Asa Gray. Under Gray's guidance Bailey developed his understanding of the plant sciences. His reputation was growing. In 1885 Michigan Agricultural College invited Liberty Bailey to return to his old school to chair the newly established department of horticulture. Gray cautioned Bailey against the move, suggesting that horticulture, as an applied science, lacked the prestige of a pure, theoretical science such as botany. Gray apparently subscribed to an intellectual hierarchy that privileged the theoretical over the applied, and he suggested that if Bailey accepted the position, he would fall into obscurity. Later that same year, having taken the job, Bailey published his first book, *Talks Afield: About Plants and the Science of Plants*.

Bailey's move to Michigan figured as only the beginning of what would be an impressive career. Three years later, in 1888, Cornell University called on Bailey, enticing him to leave Michigan to establish a department of horticulture at Cornell's Agricultural College. This represented for Bailey the opportunity of a lifetime. In that position he would be able to design a program and develop the study of horticulture in the manner he envisioned. Having accepted the job, Bailey continued to gain prominence in his work and academic leadership. In 1903 he advanced to the position of dean of the College of Agriculture at Cornell, a role he maintained until his retirement in 1913. During his tenure as dean, he became increasingly involved in the Country Life Movement and served as the chairman of President Theodore Roosevelt's Commission on Country Life, which was formed in 1909.

Bailey wrote prolifically throughout his life. From 1885 to 1903, during his professorships at Michigan and Cornell, Bailey published articles, pamphlets, and books concerned primarily with horticulture and nature study in the elementary and secondary schools. As dean at Cornell, he expanded his interests to include issues relevant to a broader and more diverse audience—topics such as science and agricultural education, public policy surrounding agriculture and the environment, and the improvement and preservation of farms and the lives of those involved with farming. Yet even as he was expanding the scope of his interests, he continued his work in horticulture.

After retiring from Cornell, Bailey settled into a more philosophical writing pattern, authoring books in which he sought to describe his vision of the world, the ways that agriculture should be practiced and—more central to this discussion—the ways that humans should regard their relationship with the world they inhabit. Bailey's preoccupation in later life with the philosophical and ethical relationships with nature seems to have been the consequence of his lifelong involvement with the plant sciences and farming.

THE CRY that resounds through Bailey's body of work is the importance of coming to know the nonhuman environment through experience in the field. He advocates nature study for children as a means of cultivating in them an appreciation for the nonhuman world and of nurturing their spiritual connection with it.[4] While he suggests that nature study is to be valued for its intangible benefits to the child, he also looks to the ways that scientists study nonhuman nature—advocating, for example, that plants be studied in their native settings so that scientists can enhance their understanding of how plants interact and depend on surrounding physical and biological elements of a particular environment. Bailey suggests that by confining their studies to the laboratory, scientists risk envisioning the world from a purely intellectual and abstract perspective. His "ecology" is one of people and plants. He advocates science as a means of better harnessing nature for human ends, but he is always highly sensitive that an imprudent use of nonhuman nature may be detrimental to the very entities upon which humans rely for their well-being.

Like Hamlin Garland, Bailey reveals a sensitivity to the nonhuman environment that was likely shaped by his boyhood experiences in the rural Michigan woods, where he was known for his solitary rambles. Bailey admits that as a child he was infused with a wonder for the mystery of the natural realm of which he regarded himself a part. In *The Nature-Study Idea* he reflects on his own childhood to illustrate how young people might learn and become involved with the classroom of nature. In recollecting his experience of a brook near his home, for example, he reveals how he learned about the environment he inhabited:

> I longed for the earthy smell when the snow settled away and left bare brown margins along its banks. I watched for the suckers that came up from the river to spawn. I made a note when the first frog peeped. I waited for the unfolding spray to soften the bare trunks. I watched the greening of the banks and looked eagerly for the bluebird when I heard his curling note somewhere high in the air. (124–25)

Bailey includes this lyrical description as a way of establishing a rhetorical foundation for the way that one can appreciate even seemingly mundane landscapes. He marvels that as a child, he took great delight in the brook during spring and summer but tended to ignore it as barren and moribund in winter.

This emphasis on childhood experience suggests that such an appreciation for nonhuman nature is innate and should be nurtured. Bailey hopes to persuade his readers that even the seemingly ordinary aspects of one's surroundings might offer insight, if one only develops the art of observation and brings a mindful awareness to a scene. Those who cannot realize some sense of appreciation or wonder for a winter scene are merely ignorant. In a leaflet titled *How the Trees Look in Winter* (1899) Bailey writes: "the winter is not lifeless and charmless. It is only dormant. The external world fails to interest us because we have not been trained to see and know it" (297). His message here is directed at the farmer who is often housebound during the winter, but his lessons would have nonetheless been meaningful to anyone living in the northern latitudes.

Bailey explicates his philosophy surrounding the value of nature study in the 1890s and early 1900s in pamphlets published as guides to teachers. He explains the benefits of nature study, suggesting that

> Nature-study, as a process, is seeing the things that one looks at, and the drawing of proper conclusions from what one sees. Its purpose is to educate the child in terms of his environment, to the end that his life may be fuller and richer. Nature-study is not the study of a science, as of botany, entomology, geology, and the like. That is, it takes the things at hand and endeavors to understand them, without reference primarily to the systematic order or relationships of the objects. It is informal, as are the objects which one sees. It is entirely divorced from mere definitions, or from formal explanations in books. It is therefore supremely natural. It trains the eye and the mind to see and to comprehend the common things of life; and the result is not directly the acquiring of science but the establishing of a living sympathy with everything that is. ("What Is Nature-Study?" 11)

In nature study for children, Bailey privileges an intuitive and emotive experience of nonhuman nature over an objective and scientific one. In speaking to an understanding of "the things at hand," without reference to "systematic order," he seems to subordinate a positivistic, scientific approach to children's nature study in favor of an approach that emphasizes an emotional apprehension of the world. Bailey argues that an understanding of nonhuman nature may reside in personal experience and that intuition and feelings are legitimate human faculties that should be employed in the ways that we engage with the world. On numerous occasions Bailey repeats the Emersonian theme that to know nature is to know oneself, and he suggests that in understanding the nonhuman dimensions of the world, the child develops a clearer sense of his or her own existence. As Bailey expounds in a 1903 essay titled "The Nature-Study Movement," the effort to bring children to the study of nature is an

outgrowth of an effort to put the child into contact and sympathy with its *own* life. . . . It would seem to be natural and almost
inevitable that the education of the child should place it in
intimate relation with the objects and events with which it
lives. . . . [O]ur teaching has been largely exotic to the child . . . it
has begun by taking the child away from its natural environment. (21; italics mine)

Bailey is not greatly concerned with the nuances of philosophical
questions that consider the place of humans in a larger nature; to
ask whether humans are continuous with or distinct from the
nonhuman realm is shortsighted. For Bailey, humans enjoy a dual
relationship with nature and are capable both of adopting an
intellectual distance from nonhuman entities that will facilitate
their study and of adopting an intuitive or emotional engagement
with these entities that allows for an integration. Nature study
encourages children more fully to appreciate the subtleties of the
world they inhabit, an awareness that in turn encourages in them
an understanding of the self as an entity existing within the whole
of creation. Indeed, one might regard as anthropocentric this utilitarian interpretation of nature as a tool toward human spiritual
growth, but herein Bailey resonates with Emerson as he suggests
that nature may be defined in manifold ways and thus that the
human experience of it may be similarly multiple and endless.[5]

Bailey develops a theme that posits a continuity between humans and the nonhuman world as he gradually discards Cartesian binaries that posit a separation between the self and nature.
"Man," he writes, "also is an animal" (*NSI* 108)—that is, an entity
within the larger realm of nature. Human beings can experience
nature not only on a physical plane but also on an intellectual
plane. In arguing that humans are animals, Bailey suggests that
nature is as much an interior human attribute as it is an external
nonhuman reality.

The ability to observe, internalize, and integrate experiences
about the world can be nonscientific, perhaps even nonrational,
and is no less valid as a form of apprehension than a critical,

scientifically based approach to studying and understanding creation. Bailey is critical of a tendency among scientists to diminish the importance of intuition and emotion in studying nonhuman nature. In an anecdote that resonates with postmodern feminist critiques of science, Bailey describes his experience at a teacher's conference at which a female teacher describes with great enthusiasm how she introduced her students to nature study by collecting plants and insects. Bailey was annoyed by a male audience member who denounced the woman's instruction as illogical and unsystematic because she failed to teach students the scientific names of the collected specimens and to situate them within a larger taxonomy. Bailey observes that the scientific approach to studying nature is legitimate, but he also argues that it does little toward fostering a child's affection and pleasure in nature. He contends that the teacher, appealing to the natural curiosity children take in the world, "approached the subject from the human side" (*NSI* 93). Bailey allows for the introduction of emotion and rejects logical positivism in science study for children.[6]

In considering how nature might be "interpreted," Bailey argues for a recognition of the intuitive and subjective experiences with the nonhuman realm, but he does not stop there. He also argues that we may enjoy a creative and artistic experience of nature and effectively adopt a lyric approach to understanding nature. "There can be no objection to the poetic interpretation of nature," he says; "In teaching science we may confine ourselves to scientific formulas, but in teaching nature we may admit the spirit as well as the letter" (121). He argues that nature poetry may enable a young student to understand the unique features of plants that might be lost if that child were forced to memorize taxonomic facts. Moreover, he argues against the notion that science alone is the source of undeviating and irrefutable truth: "What is called the scientific method is only imagination trained and set within bounds. Compared with the whole mass of scientific attainment, mere fact is but a minor part, after all. Facts are bridged by imagination. They are tied together by the thread of speculation" (*NSI* 121). Bailey contends that we can accurately describe the world only through the use of both rational and intuitive faculties; to consider the world through only one of these faculties is to perceive it in a limited way. Just as an unbridled imagination cannot provide us with an accurate description of reality, neither can a purely scientific approach that denies our emotional and spiritual experience of what we observe. Interpretation is necessarily subjective, an intellectual yoking-together of ideas, observations, and measurable conditions. An exclusively objective and scientific interpretation of the world carries with it the risk of spiritual impoverishment: "Science can never save a soul" (*Seven Stars* 115).

Though Bailey's philosophy about humans and their relationship to the world they inhabit will mature in later works like *The Holy Earth* (1915) and *The Seven Stars* (1923), he explicates that philosophy most clearly in *The Nature-Study Idea*, a book published in 1903 while he was still teaching at Cornell University. Here, within the ostensible purpose of defining the underpinnings of the nature-study movement that was gaining popularity in schools, Bailey criticizes what we might call the commodification of nature, the tendency to see elements of nature in fragments, as might be reflected in the American affection for cut flowers. It is not enough to like the flower, he argues; one must know and love the entire plant to have "a deeper hold on nature" (98).

Bailey is critical of a tendency characteristic of Judeo-Christian thought to interpret the world as a resource for human use: "The notion that all things were made for man's special pleasure is colossal self-assurance. It has none of the humility of the psalmist, who explained, 'What is man, that thou art mindful of him?'" (100).[7] Bailey is hardly anti-Christian; rather he is objecting to instrumental explanations for the existence of nonhuman creation.[8] His resistance to instrumentalism is apparent in *The Nature-Study Idea* and is openly invoked in a chapter bearing the prickly title "Must a 'Use' Be Found for Everything?" He suggests that we bring common sense to arguments that posit the existence of all creation for human good exclusively. In an anecdote about a farmer, Bailey offers the simple man's position: "But there are more homely reasons for believing that things were not made for man alone. There was logic in the farmer's retort to the good man who told him that roses were made to make man happy. 'No, they wa'n't,' said the farmer, 'or they wouldn't 'a' had prickers' " (100).

Throughout *The Nature-Study Idea* Bailey challenges the belief that nature has an exclusively instrumental value, as he opposes a popular misinterpretation of Darwin's theory of evolution. Bailey is obviously irritated with those who would attempt to explain every characteristic of a plant or animal as a trait that contributes to its own survival—a rather simplistic interpretation of Darwin's theory of natural selection. "Nothing is easier than to find an explanation for anything," Bailey complains (103), asserting that "one of the greatest faults with the popular outlook on nature . . . [is] the belief that every feature of plant or animal has only to look to see what that use is" (105). In perceiving nonhuman nature through this frame, people tend to focus exclusively on individual attributes or traits while overlooking the entity as a whole. "They look for hairs and miss the plant," Bailey intones; "They see the unusual and rare and overlook the common" (105). Bailey credits this effort to explain all of creation as a popular willingness to embrace Darwin's theory of natural selection. Bailey asserts that, unfortunately, in understanding concepts of adaptation, people now "look for adaptations and mimicry where there may be none." As he explains, "it does not follow that every part or feature of the organism is specially adapted" (106–07).

Bailey staunchly embraces a scientific approach to understanding the infinite variety of nature, yet nonetheless he does not consider a scientific explanation of natural phenomena to be at odds with religious faith. In *The Outlook to Nature* (1905) Bailey includes an essay entitled "Evolution: The Quest of Truth," in which he responds to critics of theologians by suggesting that the current debates between creationism and evolution are old news. Bailey seems to make a move toward uniting traditional Christian hierarchical views of nature with his own understanding of nature:

Evolution is the point of view of otherism and altruism. It was the old idea that the earth is the center of the universe: this geocentric doctrine Copernicus disproved. It was the old idea that all things exist merely to please man: this hominocentric doctrine Darwin disproved. Every animal and plant lives for itself and apparently as completely as if man had never existed. The recognition of these facts is one of the first steps toward a real regard for the rights of others, and consequently toward the elimination of selfishness and exclusiveness. Yet we still seem to think that every animal and plant was created for some purpose other than for itself, and we are always asking what every organism is "for." (272–73)

Bailey articulates a nonanthropocentric perspective, urging that his readers move beyond an anthropocentric worldview that assigns instrumental value to every dimension of creation. When he argues that creation would still continue without the presence or interference of man, he challenges Old Testament notions of human dominion over the planet. Bailey also seems to reject the idea of the "great chain of being" as well as a final cause. The components of nature exist merely to exist.

Bailey criticizes an anthropocentric view and asserts a scientific interpretation of creation as he clarifies misconceptions about evolutionary theory. He moves toward explaining his own evolving belief system:

Religion is as natural and as normal as other human activities and aspirations. It is itself an evolution. It is to be expected that our conception of God will enlarge as our horizon enlarges. This conception is of course anthropomorphic,—founded on human attributes. Evolution implies that God is not outside nature, but in nature, that he is an indwelling spirit in nature as truly as in man. He is immanent, not absent. (*Outlook* 292)

For Bailey, a deeper scientific understanding of creation will only enhance our understanding of God and our own divinity. Evoking an Emersonian transcendentalism, he brings together notions of a

God who permeates all aspects of human experience, including the nonhuman realm of nature. Bailey offers an updated interpretation of Emerson's idea that nature is an entity through which humans discover their own divinity. Evolution itself, as the process whereby all life forms adapt and survive, will provide evidence of God, and our understanding of that process will provide us with a closer connection to our religious and natural selves.

Bailey's position might be summarized in this observation:

> Being human, we interpret nature in human terms. Much of our interpretation of nature is really an interpretation of ourselves. Because a condition or motive obtains in human affairs, we assume that it obtains everywhere. The only point of view is our own point of view. Of necessity, we assume a starting-point; therefrom we evolve an hypothesis which may be either truth or fallacy. (*NSI* 100—01).

Bailey recognizes a fundamental conundrum that contemporary environmentalists debate. We can recognize the inherent limitations of an anthropocentric worldview, which may maximize the survival and indulgence of humans at the expense of other entities. In recognizing the problems that result from such a view, however, we attempt to envision the world in some other way, such as an ecocentric one, which does not privilege human needs and wants over the well-being of other living or nonliving entities. Yet ultimately, as Bailey suggests, we cannot escape our human perspective. At best, we might hope to temper it.

Bailey's later writings suggest that he was working toward articulating a unified vision of the relationship between human beings and nonhuman nature. Just as he was concerned with the way we appreciate nature, he also was concerned with the ways we study nature and with the effect of certain scientific methodologies on our understanding of nature.

BAILEY ADVOCATED the study of plants in situ so that we may better understand how plants and animals exist within a given environment and how those environments figure in their variation. As a plant breeder, he sought not only to produce new varieties but also to understand how plants grow and exist in specific locations. Andrew Rodgers suggests that as early as 1887 Bailey manifests an ecological view of horticulture. Bailey declares: "We need to study our plants in the field rather than the herbarium to acquaint ourselves with their entire history, and their habits."[9] He offers this view in his comments on the wild red currant, which is morphologically identical to the European wild red currant in herbarium specimens but which thrives under different conditions. When Bailey argues for considering the wider conditions under which a plant flourishes, he demonstrates his sensitivity to the mutual interrelationships of living entities—a sensitivity that informs all of his later work.

This awareness of ecology emerges openly in 1900 in Bailey's *Botany: An Elementary Text for Schools* when he includes a brief passage on ecology, defining it as "The study of the relationships of plants and animals to each other and to seasons and environments." He elaborates: "It considers the habits, habitats and modes of life of living things—the places in which they grow, how they migrate or are disseminated, means of collecting food, their times and seasons of flowering, reproduction, and the like" (226–27).[10] This attention to the relationships among plants and animals extends to humans and forms the basis of Bailey's lifelong commitment to education in natural history and the sciences. Early in his career, it is manifested in his involvement with the nature-study movement, which Bailey identifies as an effort to teach young people to see and relate to nature. It later emerges in his work in the Country Life Movement, an effort to address the conditions of rural life and the factors that cause farmers to leave the land in search of work in the cities. Bailey's concern for the loss of farmers and his recommendations for halting their exodus operates at the intersection of two of his central convictions. First, he believes that farming is an inherently positive activity on which society relies for its well-being, and second, he holds that the farmer is in a position of responsibility, not only for creating the food that society needs to survive but also for protecting and nurturing the earth that yields this food.

Bailey's belief in the connectedness of all creation finds oblique expression in his ideas about the agricultural education occurring at the university level. By 1904 he is somewhat concerned about the fracturing of science into discrete disciplines, which tends to encourage a fragmented approach to farming rather than a holistic one. In a pamphlet called *What Is Agricultural Education?* Bailey observes that the compartmentalization of agrarian study breaks it into "teachable units," which he sees as a progressive practice. He cautions, however, that such an approach to farming "tends to give a partial view of the subject":

> The larger number of farms must engage in general "mixed husbandry" rather than in specialties. Farming is a philosophy, not a mere process. The tendency of the inevitable subdividing of the subjects is to force the special view rather than the general view. (51)

This general view would be one that acknowledges that the discrete elements of agricultural education are not the end in themselves but merely the means to an understanding of the greater whole.

Bailey's concern about the risks of such a monist and positivist approach to agriculture were well-founded, given modern approaches to agricultural study, which tend to encourage a concentrated attention to discrete aspects of the farming experience.[11] In the tradition of Emerson, Bailey suggests that farming is a philosophy rather than a process. Advancing the idea of stewardship, he speaks to the ineffable spiritual dimension of a farmer's work and exposes a point of view that may not find many sympathetic listeners among modern industrial agrarians. Bailey criticizes science when it elides spirituality altogether, but he nonetheless believes in scientific method as a important tool for enhancing our understanding of nature, both human and nonhuman.

Ground-Levels in Democracy is a collection of three addresses that Bailey presented in 1915 and 1916. In one of those speeches, "The Science-Spirit in a Democracy," he considers the scientific approach as the optimal model for policy making. Science is a reliable source of "truth," a truth that is revealed through an observation of facts. Bailey suggests that science is without prejudice and is wholly objective. The "widespread teaching of science" will thus result in the development of a new public mentality rooted in objective assessment of conditions and a subsequent logical move toward right decisions. Yet when one considers Bailey's other arguments about the importance of valuing an intuitive understanding of the world, his inconsistency is obvious. In some venues he criticizes scientific approaches to nature study for the way they dampen a child's love of nature, and in others he argues that a scientific model may offer our best hope for understanding and correcting social and political problems.

In "The Science-Spirit in a Democracy" Bailey embraces an essentialist perspective about the attainment of a scientific "truth." Although he admits that an intuitive experience of nature is valid, he nonetheless confines that thought to an isolated aspect of his imagination when he discusses the role of science in resolving society's ills. He holds great hope for the role of the agricultural-experiment stations, which will bring science to farmers. By providing farmers with new knowledge that will undo old prejudices about farm practice, such stations will create an atmosphere in which the farmer "accepts the new way and begins to demand exact reasons for everything he does. Gently this attitude will work itself out in ethics, in education, in politics, in local leadership, as well as in agriculture and in commerce. Our experiment stations are laying the very foundations of democracy" (24). This point of view speaks to Bailey's efforts at persuading an audience to embrace a new view about the importance of science while he personally recognizes the problems inherent in its application to all dimensions of life.

Bailey's interest and involvement with the Country Life Movement came in the early 1900s, while he was dean of the Cornell University College of Agriculture. During this period he becomes increasingly involved in national affairs and begins to write on philosophical and political issues rather than those more directly related to nature study, horticulture, and agricultural education. In *The Country-Life Movement in the United States* Bailey calls attention to the problem of urban neglect of agriculture, arguing that attention has been focused on urban life while the plight of the farmer has been ignored. Bailey explains that the Country Life Movement is not a back-to-the-land movement concerned with relocating urban folks in rural settings. Rather, it is a movement "working out of the desire to make rural civilization as effective and satisfying as other civilization" (1). He alludes to the tendency to exhaust the land and the concern of the Country Life Movement to address this practice: "it is the immanent problem of remaining more or less stationary on our present lands, rather than moving on to untouched lands, when the ready-to-use fertility is reduced" (6).

BAILEY'S EARLY career emphasizes botany, nature study, and plant science. Following his retirement from Cornell University, his work moves into a new realm that embraces the spiritual side of his experience as a horticulturist. In 1915 Bailey published *The Holy Earth*, a work in which he discusses, in particular, the farmer's responsibility to the land. Here, Bailey most clearly details his doctrine of nonanthropocentric awareness—an appreciation for the land that results in stewardship and a sensitive reverence for its natural features. He claims that no fundamental antagonism exists between humans and nature and that "Nature cannot be antagonistic to man, seeing that man is a product of nature" (10). We are natural entities operating within, rather than externally to, a natural system—a position Bailey has assumed elsewhere in his writings in slightly different terms. He condemns the concept that there is a "bad" nature: "It is a blasphemous practice that speaks of the hostility of the earth, as if the earth were full of menaces and cataclysms" (190). If there is a fault to be assigned, it is not in the inadequacies of nature but in the failure of humans who impose inappropriate expectations on the land: "Most of our difficulty with the earth lies in the effort to do what perhaps ought not to be done" (11). Farmers fail because they attempt to farm land unsuited to that activity.

Bailey's philosophy in *The Holy Earth* is Judeo-Christian in origin, but he merges the concept of stewardship and dominion with a broader ecocentrism and an underlying skepticism about Judeo-Christian belief. "If God created the earth," he argues, "so is the earth hallowed; and if it is hallowed, so must we deal with it devotedly and with care that we do not despoil it, and mindful of our relations to all beings that live on it" (14). Bailey identifies in all of creation an "intrinsic" value, but again he waffles about the notion of dominion, suggesting that humans indeed do have control and yet must work "against our own interests" (15) toward the larger goal of protecting the earth. He contends that all which emerges from the earth is imbued with holiness and that dominion of the earth does not necessarily impart "personal ownership." He observes that we have the ability to master the earth, a fact that requires us to become more aware of our behaviors that degrade it.

As he advocates protection and reverence for the earth, Bailey condemns those practices that would degrade and destroy the planet. He faults those who are actively "digging up the stored resources" for the small kernels that contribute to the material pleasures of society. Bailey's distaste for the rising materialism of the century is expressed as disgust for the mining of natural resources:

We excavate the best of the coal and cast away the remainder; blast the minerals and metals from underneath the crust, and leave the earth raw and sore; we box the pines for turpentine and abandon the growths of limitless years to fires and devastation; sweep the forests with the besom of destruction, pull the fish from the rivers and ponds without making any adequate provision for renewal; exterminate whole races of animals; choke the streams with refuse and dross; rob the land of its available stores, denuding the surface, exposing great areas to erosion. (18)

Bailey calls for an increased attention to our wasteful and destructive habits, pointing his finger at the constituents of American consumer culture. He suggests that we should collectively be more attentive to our relationship with the earth and that this increased attentiveness might be ideally expressed in farming. Farmers should identify the natural conditions under which they are working and adapt their agricultural practices to them.

Bailey is apparently disturbed by the decrease in the number of farmers working the land and the increase in the number of large corporate farms. Concerned about the trend he observes to regard farming as a business, he cautions against losing the "capacity for spiritual contact" (24) that is inherent in farming. Bailey addresses this concern more directly in *The Harvest of the Year to the Tiller of the Soil* (1927), a book that openly challenges the increasingly technical and monist approach to farming in what is Bailey's most open attack on the expanding role of corporate agribusiness in the American agricultural scene. Here Bailey refutes the emerging paradigm of farming as exclusively a science-based process and hints at his own concerns about the impact of large-scale farming on the environment.

The Harvest is divided into two parts that structurally mirror the theoretical schism Bailey perceived between agricultural theory and practice. Bailey speaks in part 1, "The Situation," in an objective tone, offering practical comments about agriculture as a business and about where that business figures within the larger social structure, the market economy, and politics. In part 2, "The Incomes," Bailey shifts to a lyrical style as he considers farming in its more spiritual dimensions. In this section he includes chapters that address the elements and other more personal aspects of the farm experience. His chapter titles—"Wind," "Rain," "Leaves," "Weed," "Peach," and "Horse," for example—are telling. Many of these chapters are very short and provide little more than a cursory consideration of the topic. But they stand out as moments in which Bailey indulges his literary inclination, providing us with a brief view of his emotional engagement with that particular topic. Together the two sections of the book reflect the tension between

Bailey's romantic appreciation for farming and his understanding of it as a business implicated in a larger social machine. They also reflect a distinctly environmental perspective surrounding farming and Bailey's fear that as farming is increasingly dominated by corporate interests, concern for the land itself will decline.

Bailey opens *The Harvest* by setting the scene—farm country in April, an environment teeming with life:

> the juncoes are in the open fields. . . . [T]he bluebirds have come. . . . The pussy willows begin to show. . . . The winter wheat makes patches of emerald in the distance. . . . We can see where the rabbits have gnawed the bushes above the snow line. Soon we shall be looking for hepaticas; and even now the alders in the swamps are showing their tassels. (3)

This is a landscape bursting with life, and it is a life that mingles human domestic presence with the nonhuman. For Bailey, human activity on the land is as much a source of inspiration and pleasure as the renewal of nature in the springtime. The farmer reads the signs of spring evident in the land, responding to seasonal change in much the same way that plants and other animals do. The farmer responds to the smell of freshly turned earth: "It is a creative perfume that suggests teams afield, growing crops the very essence of the romantic earth. . . . [I]t will be an aroma stronger than the balm of pine woods or the wild tang of the sea" (4).

Bailey believes that this somatic response to springtime smells, and particularly the smell of warming earth, is integral to the spiritual condition of the farmer. As he explains his goal in writing *The Harvest*, he considers that the farming experience is complex, that it is more than merely a business: "There must be the proper ratio or equivalence between the money income, the intellectual satisfactions, and the expression of the soul" (7). Farming is an activity that entails more than the simple manipulation of the land; it is also an activity of the spirit.

Bailey distinguishes the farmer from what he calls a "lander," a figure who exploits the land for financial gain without considering how it might be conserved to ensure that it will continue to provide. Bailey argues that sustainable farming entails a commitment to the land: it "is a continuing occupation, year after year and perhaps generation after generation; the capital stock, which is the soil, increases in value through the effort of the farmer. There is an attachment between the man and the land. . . . [It] lies in the realm of the emotions, as deeply set as the convictions of religion" ✓ (8). This deep sense of attachment to the land, which can be created when a family farm is passed from one generation to the next, is lost when the farm is perceived as little more than a resource for food production.

Bailey is himself prophetic as he anticipates the changing shape of the American economy and the place of agriculture in it:

> It is said that in the future we are to have corporation farms of 5,000 acres and more. Perhaps; this prophecy regards farming only as an industry. If so, the world will be ruled entirely by corporations, agricultural, industrial, commercial, professional, for the corporations would control government: we shall have a government of corporations rather than of persons. Farm workers will then be operatives. (83)

OUR WORLD TODAY

Bailey cannot envision the realities of agriculture seventy years into the future and instead speculates about the potential problems of a corporate approach to farming. He concedes that some crops indeed lend themselves to cultivation on large-scale farms, and he acknowledges that problems may well be "mechanical and engineering" in character and, as such, can be overcome. Yet he also counters this admission with a cautionary note: "but the biological factors finally overtake and master the mechanical, for fertility must be maintained and this requires something in the nature of diversification and varying practice and close adaptation to local conditions" (84–85). He is confident that the family farm cannot ultimately be replaced by the corporate farm, that human needs will supersede corporate needs: "human units will remain more important than commercial units." Deeply convinced of the value of the spiritual dimension of farming and the human affinity for nature, Bailey cannot seriously ponder the specter of giant corporate farms. "Do those prophets who would industrialize all production really wish to take the farm out of the family? Factories are essentially alike anywhere. Farms are as diverse as the valleys, hills, and plains" (85). Bailey seems to align farms with a larger natural world, which is highly diverse and varied by region. The agribusiness farm he imagines would lose that idiosyncratic diversity characteristic of the small family farm.

The Holy Earth and *The Harvest* are Bailey's philosophical tracts. Both books speak to the relationship between humans and their environment, and in both, Bailey can be variously pedantic, quirky, and frankly authoritarian. Although Bailey can be eloquent and persuasive when he addresses his topic head-on, he is perhaps at his best when he transmits his message with a more subtle tone and when he indulges in his own somewhat shaky literary prose style.

That prose style is exemplified in *The Apple-Tree* (1922), which opens lyrically as Bailey muses about the absence of the apple tree in tropical climates, where he often traveled in his later life:

> The wind is snapping in the bamboos, knowing together the resonant canes and weaving the myriad flexile wreaths above them. The palm heads rustle with a brisk crinkling music. Great ferns stand in the edge of the forest, and giant arums cling their arms about the trunks of trees and rear their dim jacks-in-the-pulpit far in the branches. (7)

He sets the exotic tropical scene with a somewhat romantic description of the plant life, only to lead us back to the familiar ground of the American farm: "Yet one day it came over me startlingly that I missed the apple-tree, the sheep, and the milch cattle!" (8). Bailey uses this moment to segue into a consideration of the apple tree as a symbol of domestic spirituality, even as it can be an object of empirical scrutiny—something whose essential character can be understood through scientific observation. His study of the apple tree suggests that a human spiritual affinity with a nonhuman entity results from an intimate familiarity with that entity. In *The Apple-Tree* Bailey asserts through anecdote, observation, and lesson that the way we apprehend the world and its entities affects our behavior.

The Apple-Tree—a blend of scientific fact, horticultural advice, and lyrical commentary on the nature of the apple tree—is an implicit example for how spiritual sensitivity to nature might be compatible with scientific practice.[12] In the chapter titled "Citizens of the Apple-Tree," Bailey considers the tree as an entity within a concentric nest of interdependent communities. "The apple-tree," he tells us, "is not single in its denizens. No plant lives alone" (89). The tree figures within a larger community of other plants, animals, and insects, and it is through knowing these other entities that one gains a greater understanding of the character of the apple tree: "one cannot understand the apple-tree unless one knows something of its citizenry" (89)—those denizens to which Bailey alludes being the insects and, in particular, the offensive codling moth.

Bailey carries us through a discussion of the codling moth, introducing us to its life cycle, its habits, and its relationship to the apple tree. Explaining the balance between worm and apple, he tells us that "the worm in the apple has a delicate and interesting history. From egg to imago the transformations proceed with regularity, and they are marvelous. . . . [T]hat the moth in the air should come from a crawling worm in an apple is indeed one of the miracles of nature" (93). Bailey moves from an objective, scientific stance to a more tentative and subjective position to consider a divinity underlying creation, a divinity that infuses with meaning even the most ordinary and perhaps troublesome entity associated with apple culture. Bailey is ambivalent about the life cycle of the worm. His detailed explanation about the habits of the moth finally evolves into a lesson on the management of the codling moth by both organic and nonorganic means.

As we move with Bailey through this intimate portrait of the tree and its denizens, we learn the various controls that a farmer might bring to his orchard toward the goal of controlling the codling moth. Bailey suggests the best time for spraying arsenic compounds but also mentions an older, more time-consuming and labor-intensive organic method. He concludes his discussion of the codling moth with a more tentative observation about the human management of apple orchards:

> If man has dominion and if he needs apples, then is he within his rights if he joins issue with the insects. Yet is the insect as interesting for all that. I think we should miss many of the satisfactions of life, and certainly some of the disciplines, if there were no insects. My apple-tree is a great place for a naturalist. (93)

Bailey is caught between two views and avoids endorsing the doctrine of dominion. He suggests that if the view that man exercises dominion over the earth is correct, then we are, in a larger Lockean universe, within our rights to exercise control over that tree and its citizenry of unwanted insects.[13] Yet he undermines this view as he shifts his focus to the insects, seeming to defend them though never quite taking their side.

Bailey's implication is that the insects might also have rights within the larger natural order. His justification for our observation and awareness of insects lies in their instrumental value, which relates not to a material world but to a spiritual and emotional one: insects inhabiting apple trees are interesting and, if observed, can be a source of human satisfaction. The spiritual instrumental value in understanding the relationship between the insect and the tree must be balanced with the material instrumental value of the apple. By extension, the optimal state for farmers would seem to be one in which they recognize the divinity of the codling moth even as they eradicate it, bringing a mindful awareness to the significance of their agricultural practices.

Bailey also brings a distinctly Thoreauvian habit of mind to his ✓ consideration of the apple tree and its various perceptual dimensions. In the chapter titled "The Brush Pile," he approaches the mundane jumble of branches that remain after the apple tree is pruned, considering it as a semiological puzzle that can be deciphered to bring greater understanding to the reader:

> Today I visited the brush pile back of the orchard. Here the trimmings of the winter are placed, waiting to be burned when dry. How many are the archives that will be destroyed! Here are histories in every bud and twig and scar, of the seasons, of the accidents and deaths, the records of the tree as there are records of families.
>
> These records are not written in numbers or in letters, nor yet in hieroglyphs; yet are they understandable. Alphabet is not needed, and the key is simple. (27)

From this starting point he launches into a detailed explanation of how to read the signs of an apple tree—how to learn the significance and meaning of each bud, each shoot, each branch. Although it is spring and the branch has lain on the ground through winter, Bailey insists that "we can read it" (27). He thus carries us, step by step, through the reading. After anchoring us in the present moment, May 1921, he moves to the next point in time: "The terminal shoot is obviously of 1920; we shall name it No. 1." His analysis includes close observation of the branch—a consideration of its growth patterns and the relationship and distance between the various buds in their placement on the branch and the characteristics that distinguish them from the buds of other fruits.

Bailey continues carrying us back in time, explaining that "We cannot understand this simple unbranched terminal twig (No. 1) until we know what took place last year. A year ago, in the spring of 1920, a terminal bud that had formed in 1919 expanded and gave rise to this rapidly growing shoot" (29). His analysis and description of the branch continues in this way, slowly directing us down the branches back in time to 1917. At the point at which the branch was severed from the tree, Bailey cannot trace the history of the tree any further. He pauses to consider the numbers of leaves that the branch has generated over three years, probably

"340 leaves in total" (33). He estimates that the branch has borne "150 flowers," which have likely yielded "three or four maturing fruits" (34).

From here he moves to considering how to read other signs in the branch, which point to the way it was placed in the tree:

> It must have been upright or very nearly so, for the main axis is essentially straight and the branchlets are about equally developed on all sides; moreover, there is no indication in the bark that one exposure was the "weather side." The big twig . . . apparently found a light and unoccupied space into which to develop. . . . I suppose, however, that my branch was not topmost in the tree; there is no indication in a very long growth or strong upward tendency of the branchlets to mark the branch as a "leader." (34)

In this way, Bailey teaches his readers to read the overlooked ✓ features of an orchard. He suggests that there is much to be learned through the careful habit of observation and that such observation leads to a richer experience of the world: "These lessons gave meaning to trees and seasons. . . . I come back to a bare twig with all the joy of youth. The records of the years are in these piles of brush" (35).[14]

Bailey hints at his nostalgic connection to the apple tree as a record of the passing years. His attachment to the tree is as a symbol of domestic continuity, a living connection between humans and the world they inhabit. He also considers the symbolic meaning of various other trees, suggesting that "maples and elms are of the fields and roadsides" and are generally left uncultivated by humans, while "apple-trees are of human habitations and human labor"—the apple tree is "characteristically a home-tree" (10–11). Bailey brings his own associations to the study of this tree, envisioning it in a habitat of farm houses and outbuildings, as a part of a scene of agrarian domesticity whose passing he laments. The apple tree is a calendar and clock, providing a mark of order to human existence: "Life does not seem regular and established when there is no apple-tree in the yard . . . no orchards blooming in the May and laden in the September." Like a prodigal he promises himself that "when I reach home I shall see the apple-tree as I had never seen it before" (9), appreciating it with the fresh eye of one who has previously taken it for granted.

✓ *The Apple-Tree* suggests how one might integrate daily practice with spiritual mindfulness. Bailey brings his knowledge to a domesticated fruit tree to reveal how one might discover a vast spiritual and emotional connection to nature and look to a seemingly ordinary aspect of the landscape for manifold lessons about the way that all of nature is connected. In focusing on the apple tree, Bailey offers an example to both farmers and nonfarmers, for even many urban homes have such a tree. He also indulges in a nostalgia for a way of life that is disappearing from his world. In *The Apple-Tree* this nostalgia is gentle and contemplative.

✓ A year later in *The Seven Stars*, that nostalgia emerges as a bitter criticism of modern life, which Bailey regards as detrimental to both the planet and the human spirit. If one wished to inquire into Bailey's state of mind in his later life, *The Seven Stars* might function as a lens through which one could focus on his personal philosophy and his forty years of written work. In 1923 Bailey was sixty-five years old. Ten years earlier, he had retired from his post as dean of Cornell University's College of Agriculture, and in the intervening years he had written several short volumes devoted to elucidating his philosophy of the earth.

✓ It would be fair to suggest that Liberty Hyde Bailey may have harbored literary aspirations in which he did not indulge until later life. *The Seven Stars* and a collection of his poetry titled *Wind and Weather* (1916) were published only after Bailey had established himself as a scion of modern plant science and a leader in agricultural education. It is most likely that neither of these books would ever have been published had they been written by a man of lesser fame. *The Seven Stars*—described by Peter Schmitt as "a cryptic little volume" (xxv)—is indeed a curious work, if not in its convoluted plot, then certainly in its vague and confusing central character, Questor. Bailey projects onto this character many of his own concerns, including the intrusion of technology into modern life and the loss of "basic values" as a central force undermining the stability of society. While he is a conservative on issues surrounding social change, Bailey is progressive on environmental issues, and in *The Seven Stars* he puts forth ideas that have now, eighty years later, found wide currency—ideas like the value of urban planning to preserve natural beauty and the importance of recognizing society's collective role in environmental degradation.

The Seven Stars is a fitting book on which to conclude this discussion of Bailey. Though few would read it for entertainment, it provides a marvelous insight into Bailey as a man as it repeats the themes he preaches throughout his life. Here he reveals his stern distaste for the amusements and diversions of modern culture while demonstrating something of an egotism about his own skills as a writer. Bailey unleashes all of his inhibitions in *The Seven Stars*, indulging in diatribes on any social issue that crosses his line of vision as he critiques capitalism, motion pictures, women's fashion, the deterioration of the countryside, and the loss of a "standard" aesthetic.[15]

Bailey's message here is serious. He attempts to write a narrative that centers in Questor, a young man in his twenties who has recently completed his education and is about to enter adult life. Bailey's view is retrospective. One can imagine that at age sixty-six, he is glancing back to a time forty years earlier when he himself had completed his college education and was waiting to embark on a life ahead. In a chapter entitled "Rip Van Winkle" Bailey reveals a wonder and a disorientation with regard to the modern world as he tries to envision it through the eyes of a young man living in the 1920s.

In *The Seven Stars* Bailey lodges his first implicit criticism at capitalism. He is disturbed by the way that consumer culture has defined society, creeping into every facet of American life. In walking down a city street, the narrator—who we may assume is Bailey—comments on the overwhelming wealth of material goods that can be purchased, "things in the windows, here, there, everywhere,—pans, shoes, canes, hams, false teeth, corsets, hammers, shirts, dolls, brooms, strings, garden seeds, books, clocks, spades, collars, hammocks, cigars, medicines, bath-tubs, doughnuts and pies" (18). He is troubled at the way that materialism is driving human life, becoming the focus of human activity to the neglect of the spirit. In the rush for "more," humans have lost a connection to one another and have become more concerned with the acquisition of goods than with the welfare of the community. He rants, "the holy office of this people is trade, trade, trade!" The unfortunate result of this preoccupation is that people exhibit "an indifference to the life about them" (22).

Bailey observes that among women, an essential quality of femininity is obscured by the trappings of consumer culture. His prudish distaste for female sexuality emerges as he considers the new woman of the 1920s:

> He sees women brilliant in sex-advertisement. He marvels that they are unabashed. They . . . have the evidences of well-being but carry little of the beauty of personality. Their faces are buried in paint till character and individuality are obliterated; their colors are not cosmetics daintily applied but crude gross deceptions, to make the faces appear what they are not. . . . Every action seems to be a pose. They seem to be ever unconsciously expressing deceit, deceit, deceit! (23–24)

This deception is not confined to what women wear and how they behave but is manifested throughout the culture. As Questor strolls the city streets, he observes buildings that are offensive to the aesthetic eye. "The store fronts appall him" with their "misproportion" and "inharmony." While they lack an aesthetic harmony that Bailey would perceive as beautiful, their greatest flaw is their "false fronts, with shabby construction in the rear" (44). Like women who wear makeup, these structures conceal some underlying reality as well as their true personalities.

For Bailey, the urban scene is a ghastly underworld. Questor is a Dante traveling the streets of a modern city where the demons are the promoters of commerce. The observer is visually assaulted by the "crude figures" and the "glaring gaudy irrelevant mocking colors" of advertisements. When night descends, a natural night sky of stars and moon is overwhelmed by "transplendent ghosts . . . the skeletons that have stood naked all day on the tops of great building put on a luminous flesh and dance their crude spookish antics on the sheer walls and the roofs" (28). The brazen sexuality that has overcome the urban woman has also permeated the advertising signs that light the night sky. These nonhuman enticements "to buy, to buy, to buy" are, in their essence, an "evil" (26–27).

A pastoral message is embedded in Bailey's narrative. He makes an inexplicable shift in the "Rip Van Winkle" chapter as Rip becomes the focus of the action. Rip may be conflated with Questor; both are little more than narrative vehicles for Bailey's point of view. At one point Bailey tells us, "Rip Van Winkle is astounded and confused by the things he sees" in the city (67). Rip/Questor is disturbed and uneasy in the urban realm but discovers relief and calm when he moves beyond the city into the countryside. In the next chapter, the main character becomes "Alastor," whose relationship to the subject of Percy Shelley's poem is unclear. Their similarity exists in their journeys, which carry them through a magical, mysterious, and beautiful rural realm, a place where "the soul [is] one with all eternal things,—with hills and caverns, with sleeping fields and shores, with the wind that bloweth" (70). Alastor disappears in subsequent chapters, as Questor returns. The message Bailey promotes throughout the narrative jumble is that the rural realm provides a closer access to an essential truth. Questor observes the movement of the country "folk," who "move as if part of the scene, every person at home and in his native element" (88). These people are more closely attuned to a divine order, following a pattern of work that is "determined by the sun" (89).

As Questor nears the conclusion of his journey, he ponders deeper questions: "Are we incapable of completeness? Was the human race started wrong? Have we fallen from an original state of perfection?" Bailey weaves theological questions into his analysis of the modern world. Yet ultimately it is capitalism that he blames for the fractured state of humanity. Bailey asks, "doth

Questor realize that least of all can the balance-sheets, which are only crude records of passing affairs, save a people (much less a soul) or even be a measure of its best attainments." Humans seem to have fallen during his lifetime. Bailey laments, "There is some other plane to which the race must rise" (115). Finally, however, Questor emerges from his wandering with a new hope. He receives a tome from Winnet, a female guide who advises him with a list of homilies that include

Do not be afraid of your enthusiasms.
Stand by your ideals.
Enter not the race for wealth. (160)

Bailey, through the voice of Winnet, dishes up the wisdom of the ages unselfconsciously. Questor falls to sleep and awakens to a new understanding of the world:

It is the morning of creation, with new hills, new trees, new skies, new labors. The cattle in the pasture are essential. The old man who milks is also essential; he is part of the scene. All persons are essential. . . . The harmonies are greater than the discords. Confusion revolves itself into concord; and concord is beauty.

"The meaning of life is its beauty," is the phrase that comes unawares to him. (162–63)

Bailey builds to a conclusion with an accumulation of ideas that are at best muddled. The emotional tone of the story rises as Bailey is caught in a frenzy of literary enthusiasm that brings a resolution to the troubling observations Bailey had made about the world. Questor experiences a moment of ecstatic understanding about the meaning of life and his place in the larger society—a world that has earlier been described as corrupt. In the midst of his final "meditations" Questor understands that "One does not need to look always for the highest salary or income. . . . The character of the work and the situation in which one finds oneself are the real assets" (164–65). Bailey implies that Questor will arrive at an astounding understanding of the larger meaning of material society—of the way that capitalism has infiltrated human life, degraded personal interactions, and destroyed the environment. Yet when we reach the last paragraphs of *The Seven Stars*, we are left with Questor's banal revelation: "he is arrived at his declaration: '. . . my aim is the artistic expression of life' " (165).

The Seven Stars reveals the enigma of Liberty Hyde Bailey: a man with a concern for the commonweal and an insight that is balanced with a bit of arrogance and a limited objectivity about himself. The messages he brings to the world are few and are repeated throughout his manifold publications. Bailey's genius as a botanist and horticulturist is recognized even today: his encyclopedias on the cultivation of plants are still in print. The influence of his philosophy is less well-known, yet his interest in environmental ethics is still timely, almost a century later.[16] We can look to many of the concerns regarding the environment and see his enduring relevance—in debates about anthropocentric worldviews, in concerns over sustainable agriculture, in questions over the role of the environmental education of youth as a way to prevent environmental catastrophe. Although his legacy is difficult to unearth in the great volume of material he published, Bailey's reputation as an early environmentalist should endure for the way he believed in the value of understanding nature and of regarding the land with respect and reverence.

Bailey lived well into the twentieth century. He died a century after Emerson presented his address to the Middlesex Cattle Society, having witnessed during his lifetime the transformation of agriculture from a "philosophy" to a science. Bailey consciously formulated issues of which Emerson, Norris, Smythe, and Garland were only obliquely aware. In 1858 Emerson intuitively understood that the transformation of agriculture into a business would compromise the spiritual connection to nature enjoyed by the farmer. In 1900, as Bailey was carrying Cornell University into the era of scientific agriculture, Norris conceived of farming only as a business enterprise whose "nature" was confined to a world defined by the forces of social Darwinism. At that same time, Smythe was clamoring for reclamation, believing, like Bailey, that the nation's collective good could be realized if farming were practiced by more rather than fewer people. Ironically Smythe's vision for farmers overlooked the very nature that is at the heart of farming, as he promoted a progressive view of scientific agriculture as a tool that would enable humans to transcend the limitations of nature.

In sensibility, Garland and Bailey perhaps are most similar. Garland understood the farm on a personal level, and while he was quick to condemn the social forces that shaped farming, he shared with Bailey a reverence for the natural beauty and grace that could be observed in agricultural lands. Garland was a writer, not a scientist or a politician; his observations and sentiments were contained within a literary sphere. Bailey, perhaps more than any figure considered here, crossed all the boundaries and understood the uneven conceptual land on which farming occurs. Like Emerson, he considered the way we might perceive ourselves in nature; like Norris and Smythe, the way larger social forces were altering the practice of agriculture; and like Garland, the way farm practices affected the lives of those who lived on farms. In integrating the scientific, the spiritual, the social, and the political, Bailey was truly a modern agrarian—one whose legacy continues to this day.

Afterword

THE WRITERS I consider in this book lived in an era when farming was a prevalent occupation that was esteemed as a mainstay of our society. Today few farm. If popular culture serves as a barometer of public awareness, agriculture may not even exist in the minds of most urban folk. When I first contemplated this book, I was warned away from the topic of farming. If I hoped to write a work that might interest literary scholars, let alone a popular audience, I would do well to focus on a topic with wider appeal, such as sex, fashion, consumer culture, cultural diversity, business, or maybe even wilderness. Those living in the cities and suburbs are interested in issues that define their lives, and what they eat is an issue only if they cannot find Cheerios at the supermarket or if their hamburgers induce gastroenteritis. Some folks may contemplate nature as a consumer commodity; they may enjoy glossy images of wilderness featured in coffee-table books or even support wilderness causes. But, I was told, farming is a dull subject.

While writing most of this book I lived in the Central Valley of California, one of the most productive agricultural regions in the world. I believed that those who farm still value their work for its connection to a larger nature. I also believed that we who do not farm should better understand agriculture as a practice on which we all rely. When I began this project, I had expected to find that farmers of a century ago enjoyed a close connection to nature that had been lost to modern farmers—who, I imagined, were alienated from the nature underlying their enterprise. My own scholarly efforts to support this theory were confounded, however. I discovered that farmers today, like farmers of a century ago, are as varied as any other segment of our population. Some are more attentive to the nature implicit in their enterprise than others.

Yet a single reality underscores the experience of most farmers today—the same one that exists for those described by Emerson, Garland, Norris, Smythe, and Bailey: whether they work as managers of corporate farms or even as owners of small organic-market farms, farmers engage in their work in order to earn a living. Each one of them weighs agrarian decisions on a ledger. Some consider the long-term and perhaps intangible costs of their decisions, and others look only to the quantifiable and immediate costs and profits that will be carried through the current fiscal year. Those decisions, many would argue, figure in the long-term health of the land and of our agriculture economy.

As I write this, the topsoil of farmlands continues to erode, farmers still dose their fields with pesticides and herbicides, and the corporate farmers of the Western deserts struggle against the rising salinization of their irrigated lands—lands that perhaps never should have been farmed at all. These environmental issues prevail as the larger American community remains unaware not only about where their food is grown but also of the possible long-term consequences, both to themselves and to the environment, of the methods by which their food is produced. American consumers enjoy the luxury of ignorance. Few consider whether their tomatoes are grown in Belgian hothouses or Mexican fields, whether their chickens are raised in factory sheds and fed antibiotics or allowed to range free in the open air. Despite the relative ignorance of consumers, rural farmers still wake to the same important decisions faced by their predecessors a century ago. For it is they who determine whether the food we eat is wholesome and whether their land will sustain agriculture fifty years from now. These farmers also decide whether insects, birds, reptiles, and other wildlife inhabiting their farmlands will survive.

Liberty Hyde Bailey raises issues that are as relevant today as when he considered them one hundred years ago. He waves a cautionary flag at the approach of the modern world and laments that a simpler rural culture is being supplanted by an increasingly consumer-driven urban culture. The debates in which Bailey participates have endured. The rise of the environmental movement in recent decades has tracked the expansion of an increasingly industrialized agriculture whose tools of husbandry are ever-larger machines, more potent chemicals, and genetically engineered plants and animals. The literature of agriculture has charted the changes that define agriculture itself. I do not hope to describe agrarian literature of the twentieth century, but if I were to point to writers who might continue in the tradition of Emerson, Garland, Norris, Smythe, and Bailey, I might include such writers as Willa Cather, Mildred Walker, Linda Hasselstrom, John Steinbeck, Louis Bromfield, and Wendell Berry.

Willa Cather and Mildred Walker bring a modern view to agriculture. Cather wrote in the early century, but she reflects on the same period addressed by Garland in *Main-Travelled Roads*. In *O Pioneers!* (1913) she adapts the dream of Jeffersonian agrarianism to the lives of women and immigrants. Cather's protagonist, Alexandra Bergson, guides her family through several decades of successful farming. Like Garland, Cather describes the rich experience of nature that can be realized in farming. Her heroine, however, brings progressive agrarian techniques to her endeavor. Following a pattern that will increasingly define American agriculture through the twentieth century, she gradually acquires the failing farms of her neighbors and expands her family's original homestead into a larger, prosperous enterprise.

Mildred Walker continues in Cather's tradition in *Winter Wheat* (1944), a novel about a young woman who embraces her agrarian roots to discover that her identity is derived from the Montana wheat ranch on which she was reared. *Winter Wheat* describes a woman experiencing the joys of farming and discerning a spiritual connection to the land through her work. Walker's heroine, Ellen Webb, runs a combine as she claims a traditionally masculine role in harvesting the crops. Technology makes her participation in farming possible. Cather and Walker suggest that to work the land is to know it intimately. This idea is continued by such writers as Linda Hasselstrom. In her essays in *Land Circle: Writings Collected from the Land* (1991) Hasselstrom considers ranching as the bridge between the domesticated nature that lives within the ranch itself and the wild nature that defines the ranch lands of the West.

The political fiber that runs through Frank Norris's *The Octopus* may also be found in the work of John Steinbeck. Norris examines the influence of monopolies on farmers; Steinbeck directs his focus to the migrant farm workers of the 1930s, who were exploited by farmers. All are members of a larger economy, and like many of Garland's and Norris's characters, Steinbeck's laborers enjoy little of the bounty offered by nature in the agrarian scene. In such novels as *The Grapes of Wrath* (1939), Steinbeck illustrates the failure of Jeffersonian agrarianism. The Joad family, like Garland's Jason Edwards, are victims both of their own ignorance and of a larger agrarian economy in which they are marginal participants. Their farming techniques are poorly adapted to the land; economic failure quickly follows crop failure. Steinbeck depicts the defeat of the small family farm in the twentieth century as he reveals how large farms rely on the labor of an easily exploited, itinerant work force.

Louis Bromfield, a contemporary of Steinbeck, carries agrarian writing in a different direction. His 1933 novel *The Farm* is a nostalgic, perhaps even reactionary, story of an earlier agrarian era. Bromfield's novel traces the history of a family over several generations and depicts the transformation of American culture as families move from farms to towns and immigrants bring cultural changes to communities. Bromfield, like Liberty Bailey, laments the rising materialism of American culture, which parallels the shift of population centers from the countryside to the town.

Bromfield—whose progressive position on agriculture is also reminiscent of Bailey—is best remembered today for his effort to create an ecologically sound and sustainable farm on a thousand-acre tract called Malabar Farm, which he purchased near his boyhood home in Ohio.[1] In this great experiment in sustainable agriculture, which he began in the 1940s, Bromfield applied techniques that reduced erosion and enhanced fertility while minimizing the costly inputs of pesticides and commercial fertilizers. Bromfield is a twentieth-century Jeffersonian who addresses the practical problems of farming but also believes that farming offers a way of life that can enhance the larger society. Like Liberty Bailey, he believes that the farm provides an ideal place where children might develop a "warmth and love of Nature" (2). Good citizens, he suggests, can be fostered in agrarian communities.

Wendell Berry has continued in Bromfield's tradition, uniting a personal experience in agriculture with a literary habit of mind. Berry's agrarian commentary radiates from his Kentucky farm and community, where he has lived most of his life. His work reflects an ecological sensibility that affirms human culture while nonetheless criticizing behaviors that have resulted in environmental degradation and destruction. His *Unsettling of America* (1977) is his most outspoken attack on the industrialized agriculture that boomed after World War II—a kind of agriculture that has both reflected and encouraged the further disintegration of rural agrarian communities. In his collections of essays, such as *A Continuous Harmony* (1972) and *The Gift of Good Land* (1981), he argues that the careful management of land is synonymous with the care of family and community. A knowledge of the local character of a farm region will result in a heightened concern and respect for that region. Throughout his fiction and nonfiction, Berry implicitly and explicitly calls for the practice of agriculture that centers in small farms and small communities.[2] Vast corporate farms exist only to generate profit and, as such, are not managed with a concern for the long-term health of the land. Much of Berry's work reinforces a common theme: environmental destruction, especially that associated with agriculture, is the consequence of valuing the rights of the individual over the good of the greater society.

Berry considers the idea of ecology in farming, asserting throughout his work that relationships between the individual and the community ultimately are played out in our treatment of the land. The farms that will be sustainable are small farms run by folks who have their history in the place and a vested interest in its preservation. His message is shared by other writers who, throughout the 1980s and 1990s, have called for a transformation in modern agriculture. Wes Jackson has worked to bring together sustainable agriculture and the human community at the Land Institute in Salina, Kansas. In *Becoming Native to This Place* (1994) he considers the forces in our culture that have eroded our familiarity and kinship with the land. Becoming native will require that we understand why and how American agriculture has failed—and how we have "sent our topsoil, our fossil water, our oil, our gas, our coal, and our children into that black hole called the economy" (12). He has coedited and contributed to such essay collections as *Meeting the Expectations of the Land* (1984) and *Rooted in the Land* (1996), which address and promote sustainable agriculture.

The writers who address farming today are manifold. My efforts to distinguish a few here necessarily neglects many others who write eloquently on agricultural issues or who address farm life in fiction, essay, and poetry. I might also include here the work of William Kittredge, Mark Kramer, Gene Logsdon, David Mas Masumoto, and Jane Smiley. Kittredge has reflected on Western farming and ranching and his own family's transformation of the arid land of eastern Oregon.[3] Mark Kramer explores the business of agriculture as he examines dairy and hog farming and tomato agribusiness in *Three Farms: Making Milk, Meat and Money from the American Soil* (1980). Gene Logsdon eloquently explores the issues facing small farmers in essays collected in *At Nature's Pace: Farming and the American Dream* (1994), while David Mas Masumoto quietly traces in *Epitaph for a Peach: Four Seasons on My Family Farm* (1995) the questions and problems he faced as he tried to bring organic farming techniques to his San Joaquin Valley peach farm. Jane Smiley's *A Thousand Acres* (1991) has gained acclaim as a novel of family relationships, but it deserves attention in this discussion because it also examines the economics of farming and the techniques modern Midwestern farmers are bringing to their massive industrialized "family" farms.

I regard this growing body of literature with the hope that it ✓ may reflect a greater awareness of agriculture and its central place in our existence. No doubt I have neglected some writers who deserve mention here or who may reflect on the uneven land of American farming in a way that I have overlooked. To them, I apologize. There are more books to be written on this topic, and I look forward to reading them all.

N O T E S

1. See Garland's *Main-Travelled Roads* (1891), Steinbeck's *The Grapes of Wrath* (1939), and Smiley's *A Thousand Acres* (1991).

2. For example, Susan Fenimore Cooper's *Journal of a Naturalist in the United States* (1856; first published as *Rural Hours*) offers her perspective on the countryside surrounding her home. Sarah Orne Jewett's *Country of the Pointed Firs and Other Stories* (1896) depicts women who cultivate and manage nature in their gardens and in nearby woods. For texts that deal with ranching during this period, see for example, Helen Hunt Jackson's *Ramona* (1884) and Elinor Pruitt Stewart's *Letters of a Woman Homesteader* (ca. 1910).

3. Willa Cather's work emerges late in the period on which I focus here. I regard her work as reflecting a modern sensibility; it speaks to tensions characteristic of twentieth-century rather than nineteenth-century agriculture and may better be addressed within the context of modern agriculture.

4. An example of this kind of work is John P. O'Grady's *Pilgrims to the Wild*, which explores how writers such as John Muir turn to wilderness in spiritual pilgrimages. For a more in-depth discussion of this movement see Love, "Et in Arcadia Ego." See also Sarver, "Environmentalism."

5. In *Nature and Madness* Shepard presents a speculative account of the shift in survival methods used by humans from the late Paleolithic to the Neolithic periods. Implicit in his argument is that hunting/gathering is good and agriculture is bad. See also Shepard's "Post-Historic Primitivism." In *Idea* Oelschlaeger considers the Neolithic mind and wilderness, offering a view similar to Shepard's that late Paleolithic life was inherently closer to nature.

6. See for example Naess, "The Shallow and the Deep"; Devall, "Deep Ecology Movement"; and Sessions, "Ecocentrism."

7. Ellis observes that environmental debates often center in efforts to identify a single "root cause" of environmental problems ("On the Search" 267.) One aspect of this tendency is reflected in neoprimitivists and many followers of deep ecology, who contend that the "root cause" of environmental problems is an anthropocentric world view that supported the rise of agriculture.

8. See *Practice* for Snyder's major statement on the concept of wildness.

9. A paradox in Snyder's work is that while he is implicitly critical of domestication and the loss of wildness that accompanies this process, he nonetheless supports the notion of community, especially a larger community that embraces both humans and nonhuman nature.

10. Marx considers Jefferson within a larger pastoral tradition, discussing Jefferson's agrarianism and the way in which query 19 of *Notes on Virginia* reflect an underlying pastoralism (see *Machine* 116–44).

11. Jefferson and others were aware of the relationship between deforestation and climate change; he voiced his support for the work of Lewis E. Beck in a personal letter, suggesting to Beck that plant and animal surveys "should be repeated once or twice in a century, to show the effect of clearing and culture towards changes of climate" (*Writings* 72).

12. Allen and Asselineau, *American Farmer* 34. Crèvecoeur lead an adventurous life. As a young man he traveled to Canada, where he fought in the French and Indian Wars. He later migrated to the British colonies and became a naturalized British subject in 1762. Crèvecoeur went on to marry a woman from a prominent New York family. His British loyalties, however, placed him in disfavor during the Revolution and resulted in his flight to England. He eventually returned to New York, dividing the remainder of his life between France and America. He died in 1813.

13. For an analysis of the subtextual rewriting of Crèvecoeur's *Letters* that occurs in the *Sketches*, see Robinson, "Community."

14. In *The Frontier in American History* Turner writes, "The superintendent of the census for 1890 reports . . . that the settlements of the West lie so scattered over the region that there can no longer be said to be a frontier line" (9).

CULTIVATING AN UNEVEN LAND

1. Jehlen frames this tension in more traditional and philosophical terms as a reconciliation between the "ideal and the material," suggesting

that Emerson—especially in the "Commodity" section of *Nature*—"sets the policy of refusing to distinguish between the real and the metaphoric, or the physical and the ideal" (*American Incarnation* 89).

2. Van Leer explains this passage best when he suggests that Emerson reveals that "the pursuit of a 'theory' of nature convinces only that matter is essentially inscrutable; the examination of real natural facts demonstrates that perception is the sole datum of experience." In considering that the meaning of Emerson's *Nature* resides in the interplay between content and form, Van Leer identifies an inherent tension between the first two parts of the work that points to Emerson's effort to deal with (among other concepts) Cartesian dualisms. Emerson considers a relationship with nature from both a philosophical and a personal perspective; "taken together, then, these two chapters question not the kind of relations between Descartes's two realms, but the very possibility of a relation itself" (*Emerson's Epistemology* 24). Emerson employs similar rhetorical strategies in his later work.

3. The unabridged *Oxford English Dictionary* devotes over two pages to the definitions of "nature."

4. Scudder describes Emerson as a quiet observer who took a sincere interest in his neighbors and Concord events (see *Concord* 171–73).

5. That Emerson was himself a farmer is suggested by his biographers: Rusk notes that in October of 1858 Emerson received income from the sale of a cow and of apples (*Life* 393); Allen reports that Emerson won a prize for his grapes at the annual Concord cattle show in 1859 (*Waldo Emerson* 589).

6. Because Emerson addresses his audience and readers as masculine and uses the masculine "man" to designate humans, I use a similar terminology.

7. Jehlen speaks to this tension between a spiritual and a material economy, arguing that Emerson considers nature as a material commodity, thereby absorbing "the category of commodity, of commerce and trade, into the world of the transcendent" (*American Incarnation* 90). Jehlen points to the way that Emerson's farmer can occupy both a commercial and a spiritual position in his scheme.

8. Emerson presented "Man the Reformer" to the Mechanics' Apprentices' Library Association in Boston 25 January 1841.

9. Gilmore considers Emerson's doctrine of the farm as expounding a "principle of self-sufficiency" that enables one to maintain intellectual independence (see *American Romanticism* 21). Gilmore asserts that it

reflects on Emerson's efforts to separate human experience from the marketplace. I allow that this reading may be accurate, but I think that it simplifies Emerson by minimizing his tendency to express his philosophy in metaphor. The doctrine of the farm may speak not only to Jeffersonian idealism but also to transcendental practice as it relates to nature.

10. Horwitz addresses a similar theme in *By the Law*, where he asserts that nature is a "protean rhetorical instrument" (4–5) because its value may be variously defined. Nature has been viewed as immanent, as alien and unavailable to human experience, and finally, as a value "historically forged," i.e., subject to ongoing revision within the contexts of a given historical moment (10–11). Given this range of interpretations, nature then is invoked as an authority to support sometimes conflicting discourses.

11. Corrington suggests that Emerson considers the farmer as a "living symbol of nature," and a "paradigm of how nature interacts with the human process" ("Emerson" 20).

12. Corrington defines this space as an agricultural "midworld" that fulfills the same function for Emerson as the poem—that is, both poems and farms "represent clearings within which eternal truths appear" ("Emerson" 21). Like the pastoral utopia, this space is significant for its metaphoric value as a place where spiritual work is conducted.

13. For a discussion of Jefferson's view of the role of farmers in the United States, see Griswold, "Agrarian Democracy."

14. Van Leer observes that in the famous "transparent eyeball" passage Emerson pushes away "people and community . . . in favor of the uncontained, the immortal, and the wild" (*Emerson's Epistemology* 22). Emerson achieves unity with nature by merging through transparency; simultaneously, however, he possesses the very nature into which he merges. Of key significance for me is Emerson's assertion that solitude and isolation from human communities seem to be a necessary element in achieving transcendence.

15. Brown observes that the mass production of clocks increased rapidly after 1830, making timepieces so widely available to the general population that concepts of both time and industrial efficiency were transformed (*Modernization* 134–35).

16. Passmore provides in *Man's Responsibility* the best discussion of the historical lineage of the stewardship model. For a discussion of the philosophy of stewardship in the twentieth century see Thompson, *Spirit.*

17. In "The Young American" Emerson identifies an affection that emerges from an intimate relationship with the land: "I look on such

improvements also as directly tending to endear the land to the inhabitant. Any relation to the land, the habit of tilling it . . . generates the feeling of patriotism" (*CW* 369).

18. For discussions of the changes in agriculture during the nineteenth century see Cochrane, *Development*, and Brown, *Modernization*.

19. Danhof observes that the cast-iron plow was introduced to the Northeast from 1820 to 1830 or 1835, but it was only gradually adopted. By the 1850s most farmers had replaced their wooden plows with cast-iron plows, which provided for more efficient cultivation of larger sections of land (*Change* 186–94).

20. Gilmore contends that this passage points to Emerson's abandonment of the Jeffersonian tradition evident in his earlier work and argues that farming figures as little more than a refuge from city life (*American Romanticism* 32).

21. Emerson's confidence in the potential for science to improve agriculture also is reflected in "The Young American" when he argues: "On one side is agricultural chemistry, coolly exposing the nonsense of our spendthrift agriculture and ruinous expense of manures, and offering, by means of a teaspoonful of artificial guano, to turn a sandbank into corn" (*CW* 381).

22. Thoreau modifies this theme in his discussions of the tension between the wild and the domestic. This tension appears throughout his work but enjoys its most direct explication in "Walking."

23. Oelschlaeger suggests that Emerson is "anthropocentric and androcentric" (*Idea* 134–36). Worster considers the ambiguity of Emerson's views but implicitly finds fault with Emerson's concern for the condition of humans (see *Nature's Economy* 103–07).

24. For a discussion of Christianity and anthropocentrism see Lynn White Jr., "Historical Roots." On the subject of anthropocentrism, the humanist tradition, and environmental problems, see Ehrenfeld, *Arrogance*. A wide range of texts have been published since the 1980s that articulate and promote the philosophy of deep ecology, which identifies anthropocentrism as a perceptual orientation that figures as a root cause of environmental problems. See, for example, Devall and Sessions, *Deep Ecology*, and Naess, "The Shallow and the Deep." For an overview of the critical discussions surrounding deep ecology see Sessions's anthology, *Deep Ecology*. Counterarguments to the deep ecology positions have been offered by social ecologists, most notably by Bookchin in such books as *Philosophy*.

25. Ecofeminist writing has covered a wide philosophical range. See Merchant's *Death* for one of the best-known explorations of the ways a feminine interpretation of nature resulted in an exploitative relationship that mirrored the treatment of women. See also Warren, "Power," and Biehl, *Finding*. For an overview of ecofeminist thought, see for example the essays in Plant, ed., *Healing*; Merchant, ed., *Ecology* (174–245); and Diamond and Orenstein, eds., *Reweaving*.

NATURE AND THE MIDWESTERN FARM

1. Most scholars cite Garland's autobiography, *A Son of the Middle Border*, as a primary source of information about Garland's early years in Boston. Garland describes there his thwarted effort to undertake formal study at Harvard, explaining that the "Harvard lectures were inaccessible" (322). Holloway recounts a similar tale in *Hamlin Garland*, deriving much of her information from Garland's personal account, as does McCullough in his *Hamlin Garland*.

2. Wilson considers the tendency among humans to "focus on life and lifelike processes" (*Biophilia* 1). This "innate" tendency can explain an affinity that many experience for nonhuman nature found in wilderness or, in Garland's case, the open lands of the Midwest.

3. Were he writing one hundred years later, his choice of words might resonate as bioregional in its orientation, through its privileging of a local authority and a marginalizing of a dominant, global, standard derived from European models. Garland's message, and Gary Snyder's, a century later, are rather similar. Like Garland, Snyder laments the loss of an original connection to one's local regions, and suggests that art emerges from its locale: "Each dance and its music belong to a time and place" (*Practice of the Wild* 49). This causes me to wonder if Snyder's message, while certainly modern in its focus on ecology and an emphasis on traditionally marginalized native cultures, is nonetheless a part of a much larger American tradition that calls for a "return" to some original condition, which would entail a deeper connection to the land.

4. As one who had not had the advantage of studying within the formal structure of a university, Garland critically observes, "there is no chair of English literature which is not dominated by conservative criticism, and where sneering allusion to modern writers is not daily made" (*Crumbling Idols* 11).

5. Meyer divides Garland's literary career into an early period of realism that was followed by a much lengthier period of romanticism ("Hamlin Garland" 666). Pizer divides Garland's career into three phases: 1884–95 figures as his early reform phase when he writes his middle border fiction, which is characterized by a concern for social issues; 1896–1916 marks his period of Rocky Mountain romance; and 1917–40 is the period during which Garland writes his literary autobiographies and becomes increasingly conservative (*Early Work* vii). Others such as Harrison and Ziff have recognized the romantic elements that pervade even his earliest works. This view is cited by numerous critics as the "agreed-upon" interpretation of Garland's work. Ziff suggests that Garland's ambiguous stance represents a literary predisposition to a romantic style, to which he succumbs in his later years ("Crushed" 287–88). Harrison takes a kinder view of Garland's dual style and suggests that it represents the despair and hope which is part of the "double vision of naturalism" ("Hamlin Garland" 327).

6. For a discussion of the mythic role of the farm and the figure of the yeoman farmer, see Smith, *Virgin Land*. Smith argues that the "vast and constantly growing society in the interior of the continent became one of the dominant symbols of nineteenth-century American society, a poetic idea . . . that defined the promise of American life" (123). Garland's own preoccupation with the small farmer in his early works reflects a larger popular interest in the figure. Smith suggests that by the nineteenth century, the image of the frontier farmer had acquired heroic status as the central figure in the vision of America as the garden of the world.

7. Ahnebrink suggests that Garland's early writing—works such as *Jason Edwards* and the stories of *Prairie Folks*—"comes closest to naturalism in technique and ideas" (*Beginnings* 86).

8. See Pizer, *Realism* 11–14. Pizer comes closest to articulating my vision of Garland, yet I do not embrace Pizer's tendency to identify coherence in Garland's work through the interplay of these tensions. I allow that Garland is a much more inconsistent writer than Pizer would, and I feel no necessity to read unity and coherence into works that are frankly messy in their management of disparate ideas.

9. See Howard, *Form and History*; Michaels, *Gold Standard*; and Seltzer, *Bodies and Machines*.

10. Ironically, while Garland is critical of land speculation for the way it undermines the success of the yeoman farmer, that very activity was once seen as a means of achieving success in America. Benjamin Franklin

suggested that land speculation was an appropriate method for building a fortune. In his "Information to Those Who Would Remove to America" he suggests that European immigrants of modest wealth might purchase frontier land in anticipation of its value increasing due to population growth.

11. Pizer identifies the method of taxation which Garland favored: "Land would be taxed, not in ratio to improvements, but according to the average value of the land around it. Not only would this eliminate land speculation, but it would also, because of the greatly increased land tax, free both industry and the public from all other forms of rent and taxation" (*Early Work* 38).

12. The "romanticism" I identify in Garland's work is more akin to that found in the work of the English romantics or the American transcendentalists, who attribute a spiritual connection to the landscape. Garland's work reveals little of the metaphysical or supernatural elements often associated with American romanticism.

13. This narrative tendency is repeated by Norris, who creates Presley as the character through whom we may observe the agricultural land. Like Garland's Howard McLane and Seagraves, Presley is an outsider who possesses a more sensitive eye than most people.

14. "Up the Coulee" is generally accepted as an autobiographical story that reflects Garland's own return to Iowa; the urban actor who returns to his home land is Garland himself.

THE EPIC OF CALIFORNIA AGRICULTURE

1. Norris was aware of the popular debates surrounding agriculture and their literary treatments. For example he was familiar with Edward Markham's "The Man with the Hoe," which had received wide acclaim in 1899, and it is highly likely that Norris was familiar with Hamlin Garland's stories as well. Garland writes that Markham had told him of Norris, and he writes of meeting Norris early in 1901, a few months prior to the release of *The Octopus* (see *Companions* 10).

2. For a discussion of Zola's influence on Norris see Walcutt, *Naturalism* 136–51, and Pizer, *Novels* 113–78.

3. Considering Norris's *The Responsibilities of the Novelist* and his commitment to realism, Chase observes that Norris's interest in romance

resulted in his tendency to subordinate minute detail to the deeper passions that drive characters (*American Novel* 187).

4. A generation of Norris scholars have devoted considerable energy to finding and explaining unity and coherence in the novel. Graham identifies unity in the aesthetic context (see *Fiction*). Dillingham looks to "the creative and rejuvenating powers of instinct" as the center around which the novel coheres (*Instinct and Art* 65). Others—such as Pizer, Martin, and Civello—have considered the way that Norris's philosophy provides a coherence to the novel. These wide-ranging efforts at deciphering Norris speaks to his sloppy literary style, which pulls into it a range of ideas, philosophies, and artistic theories without an adequate consideration of their interplay and larger novelistic effect.

5. To a reader familiar with the San Joaquin Valley, the presence of the mission there is ludicrous. Refuges for the Spaniards who settled Alta California in the eighteenth century, the missions in the chain running south to north from San Diego to Sonoma were spaced to allow for roughly a day's travel between them. Norris seems oblivious to the logic of the missions' original planning, but the reader who clambers with Presley "to the higher ground, on the crest of which the old Mission . . . [was] now visible" might laugh at the implications of the presence of Spanish mission in the Sierra foothills (*Octopus* 28). It suggests that wayward Spaniards became confused as they traveled north, veered to the east, crossed a wide valley, and set up housekeeping hundreds of miles from El Camino Real, where all the other missions were established.

6. Buell also explores this idea in *Environmental Imagination* (83–88), where he suggests that in fiction, the notion of setting "deprecates what it denotes, implying that the physical environment serves for artistic purposes merely as backdrop, ancillary to the main event" (85). This tendency, which Buell observes in wilderness romance, is also evident in agrarian literature.

7. Martin examines the notion of force in *The Octopus* as it relates to Herbert Spencer and his theories; see his *American Literature* for a comprehensive overview of this theme. For a study of the force concept as it relates to naturalism see Kaplan, *Power and Order*.

8. Graham argues that the stories of Vanamee, Annixter, and Presley are "expressed in three generic modes": Gothic romance, realism, and pastoralism, respectively (*Fiction* 107).

9. Addressing this philosophical conundrum in *Hand's End*, Rothenberg considers the place of technology in our conceptions of nature and

sets his analysis within the context of contemporary criticism, which posits human technology as distinct from humanity. He argues for technology as an extension of humanity. I don't suggest that Norris was necessarily consciously aware of this issue, yet it nonetheless emerges as a subtextual theme in *The Octopus*.

10. Pizer identifies a philosophical coherence in Norris, arguing that Norris's philosophy reflects the influences of evolutionary theism, particularly that promulgated by Joseph LeConte (see *Novels* 3–22). I tend to agree with Martin, however, who offers a pointed critique of Norris's muddled thinking, judging him as "absorbing ideas from second and third-rate thinkers and from the popular milieu, and [holding] these conceptions so uncritically that their shallowness and contradictions became his own" (*American Literature* 146).

11. Most critics generally concur that Norris is grappling with the second law of thermodynamics here, reflecting on the implications of the conservation of energy. Seltzer argues that this passage reflects a tension between masculine and feminine modes of production, which are played out in the discourse of thermodynamics (*Bodies and Machines* 28–29). Civello argues that force produces the wheat, which is a physical manifestation of a divine spirit; Vanamee, he suggests, offers to Presley a LeContean teleology (*Literary Naturalism* 64–65).

12. Graham considers this moment in *The Octopus* and argues that Norris is invoking Mallarmé's "L'après-midi d'un faune: églogue" in his creation of Presley (see *Fiction* 68–74).

13. Seltzer also considers Derrick within the context of mining and agriculture and the maternal earth (see *Bodies and Machines* 34).

14. Norris creates a strange vision of the farmland in book 2, chapter 2, of *The Octopus*: early in that chapter we find Hilma Tree in the lush green oasis under the trestle; we see Dyke in the green forest of his hop farm and Presley observing Vanamee in the "great wilderness of bare green hillsides" (241). Oddly, the wheat is the only plant that seems to have deferred germination: the wheat fields are still "brown" and "ruddy" at this undisclosed spring date.

15. Norris was likely aware of debates surrounding farm management. He describes Derrick as a man who cannot envision the long-term advantages of sustainable agriculture and who is as contemptuous of Annixter's practices as Annixter is of his: "The idea of manuring Los Muertos, of husbanding his great resources, he would have scouted as niggardly,

Hebraic, ungenerous" (52). For Derrick the only value in the land is immediate and short term.

16. In the Greek story of Apollo and Daphne, Apollo is smitten with Daphne through Cupid's mischief; Daphne, uninterested in Apollo, flees. She calls out to her father, Peneus, to save her. He transforms her into a laurel tree. Apollo, vowing to remain near her always, claims her as his own tree, wearing her leaves as a crown. There are some distinct parallels between the classical myth and Norris's story of Hilma and Annixter.

17. Pizer argues that in this moment Annixter "identifies the emergence of the wheat with the bursting forth of his love, since both contribute to the perpetual renewal of life" (*Novels* 128–29).

18. Norris implies a relationship between higher education and a sensitivity to nature. The two "land miners," Derrick and Dyke, are not college-educated; conversely, Presley, Annixter, Vanamee, and Annie Derrick all have had the advantage of education, and all four of them express a greater sensitivity or awareness concerning the relationship between humans and the nonhuman realm. (While it isn't clear that Annie Derrick attended college, we know that she was a school teacher, which suggests a certain level of education.)

19. This magical seed ranch is incredible in 1880 or even, as Norris writes the novel, in 1900. From the perspective of the late nineteenth century, however, Norris could be describing what one might observe in a modern agricultural factory, a greenhouse where plants are manipulated by growers to bloom unnaturally—a place, artificially lighted at night, where colors are indeed visible in darkness.

20. Although he published "The 'Nature' Revival in Literature" in 1903, Norris quite likely was aware of and familiar with the nature writing that was emerging from both California and New York. Hamlin Garland mentions dining with both Norris and Ernest Thompson Seton at the home of Juliet Wilbor Thompkins 20 January 1901 (*Companions* 11).

THE DRAMA OF RECLAMATION

1. Parts 1, 2, and 3 of the first and second editions of *The Conquest* are essentially the same. Part 4 of the first edition is titled "The Army of the Half-Employed," suggesting Smythe is focusing on the application of his vision to social causes; part 4 of the second edition is titled "The Triumph of the Movement," reflecting the successful passage of the Newlands

Reclamation Act in 1902 and a refocusing of Smythe's energies. The two fourth parts are substantially different from one another. In the second edition Smythe shifts his focus from plans for cooperative farm colonies to documentation of new reclamation efforts and includes a chapter addressing the spiritual dimension of reclamation.

2. See "Smythe," *National Cyclopedia*, and Harriet B. Smythe, "Biographical Sketch."

3. It is worth emphasizing that Smythe was not a farmer, though he can certainly be included among the class of people whom Hofstadter has described as believing deeply in the goodness of agriculture and promoting the agrarian myth (*Age of Reform* 25).

4. For a discussion of the Populist movement, see McMath, *American Populism*; Hicks, *Populist Revolt*; and Hofstadter, *Age of Reform*.

5. For the standard discussion of the nineteenth-century tension between the myth of the "Great American Desert" and emerging myth of the great garden of the American West, see Smith, *Virgin Land*, chap. 16.

6. Crèvecoeur suggests that a rough class of citizen comprised the first wave of settlers, who made safe the wilderness for "a second and better class, the true American freeholders" (*Letters* 79). This interpretation of history as occurring in stages also resonates with the work of Frederick Jackson Turner. For a similar cavalcade-like rendering of American history see Turner's "The Significance of the Frontier in American History," written in 1893 (see *The Frontier* 1–38), and "The Problem of the West," which appeared in the *Atlantic Monthly* in September 1896. Smythe differs from Turner in that he eliminates Native Americans and other ethnic groups from his history.

7. Smythe's vision of history may be one that he modified or adapted from Andrew Carnegie, whom Smythe has cited as an influence. Wall observes that in *Triumphant Democracy* Carnegie "sought to prove his basic thesis that the United States was rich, progressive, and capitalistic because of the political order that had been established in 1787" (*Carnegie Reader* 207). Although capitalism does not overtly enter Smythe's discussion, this link may explain his somewhat arbitrary choice of the surrender of Cornwallis at Yorktown as the beginning of American history.

8. Smythe is engaged in a writing of history as a narrative. For a consideration of the ways that the narrative form can effectively manipulate our understanding of history, see Hayden White, *Content* 1–25.

9. Smythe's uneasiness about the influx of poor non-Anglo-Saxon people is suggested by the books he cites as sources of his inspiration: In the

first edition of *The Conquest*, he cites Douglas Campbell's *The Puritan in England, Holland, and America*, Andrew Carnegie's *Triumphant Democracy*, and M. Edmond Demolins's *Anglo-Saxon Superiority*. Demolins's book, translated from French, attempts to explain the social institutions and practices that earned for the Anglo-Saxons their superior status in the world.

10. Smith offers the similar observation that "Americans were used to judging the fertility of a new land by the kind of trees growing on it"; the absence of trees suggested that "the area was unsuited to any kind of agriculture and therefore uninhabitable by Anglo-Americans" (*Virgin Land* 175).

11. For a discussion of the way that irrigation figured in the decline of fertility in ancient Mesopotamia, see Hillel, *Out of the Earth* 78–87.

12. John C. Van Dyke's *The Desert* was published in 1901, and Mary Austin's *Land of Little Rain* in 1903. While it is impossible to know Smythe's motivation for including his new chapter in his 1905 edition, the inclusion of a distinctly spiritual dimension may be explained by a rising popular interest in the aesthetic and spiritual aspects of desert lands, to which Smythe may be responding.

13. Americans have traditionally laid claim to large tracts of land with speculation in mind. Cochran observes that "Each pioneer family tried to acquire as much land as it could by legal means, or otherwise. . . . Then, the pioneer family tried to sell the improved farm to a land-hungry family with some ready cash in the succeeding settlement wave" (*Development* 183–84). Thorstein Veblen was critical of this practice because it resulted in absentee ownership, and a dependence on hired labor. He also suggested that the tendency to acquire as much land as possible for speculation resulted in an increased reliance on equipment to farm the land, which was obtained at the cost of borrowing money, which ultimately resulted in higher farm production costs (see *Absentee Ownership* 129–41).

14. See Garland's *Main-Travelled Roads* and *Prairie Folks* for ficitionalized critiques of the status of farm women. Bailey, who chaired the Country Life Commission, discusses the difficult conditions facing farm women in the commission's *Report* for the year 1909.

15. Smythe may be hinting at a belief in environmental determinism. He implies that humans respond to the environment, which exerts an influence on humans. This concept resonates with the language of Frederick Jackson Turner, who linked the frontier environment with the

development of American civilization. Turner suggested: "The history of our political institutions, our democracy, is not a history of imitation . . . it is a history of the evolution and adaptation of organs in response to changed environment, a history of the origin of a new political species" ("The Problem of the West" 205–06).

16. Thomas S. Kuhn introduced the concept of paradigm shifts in science in *The Structure of Scientific Revolutions* (1962). His ideas have been adopted by environmentalists, particularly advocates of the deep ecology perspective, who speak to a paradigm shift in human values as a necessary element in averting environmental disaster. For social applications of Kuhn's theories see Capra, *Turning Point*.

17. For a discussion of the various state modes as they relate to irrigation see Worster, *Rivers* 17–60.

18. For a discussion of the New Paradigm movement of the 1980s see Zimmerman, *Contesting* 57–90.

19. See Berry, *Unsettling of America*, and Jackson, Berry, and Colemen, eds., *Meeting the Expectations*, both of which works suggest that the personal interest associated with ownership of small farms results in a more careful management of agrarian land.

NATURE, SCIENCE, AND AGRICULTURE

1. Schmitt characterizes Bailey as a nature lover who "contributed to the Arcadian mystique" (*Back to Nature* xxii). Bowers describes Bailey as an "agrarian sentimentalist" (*Country Life Movement* 45).

2. For a criticism of absentee ownership and technological large-scale farming see Berry, *Unsettling of America*.

3. This and all subsequent biographical information is derived from Rodgers, *Liberty Hyde Bailey*, and Dorf, *Informal Biography*. Much of Dorf's material seems to be drawn from Rodgers's earlier work.

4. Bailey's concern to engender in mankind an appreciation for nonhuman nature is one that has persisted in today's environmental movement. See, for example, Nabhan and Trimble, who suggest in *Geography of Childhood* that "wild" places should be preserved as areas where children may discover a connection to nature.

5. Bailey was likely familiar with at least Emerson's *Society and Solitude*; in *The Nature-Study Idea* he quotes Emerson's advice in "Civilization," to "hitch your wagon to a star" (14).

6. Postmodern critiques of science take their analysis to a considerably deeper and critical level. Keller, for example, argues against a tendency to divide the world into subject and object, a habit that is reflected in the way modern science is practiced: "in characterizing scientific and objective thought as masculine, the very activity by which the knower can acquire knowledge is also genderized. The relation specified between knower and known is one of distance and separation. It is that between a subject and object radically divided, which is to say no worldly relation" ("Gender and Science" 191).

7. Bailey's criticism of such instrumentalism is not to be equated with similar critiques made later in the century by environmental theologists like Lynn White Jr., who argued that all of our environmental problems could be traced to a Judeo-Christian world view (see "Historical Roots").

8. Bailey's biographers offer little information about his religious upbringing; however, his larger philosophy is entirely compatible with Protestant Christianity and his allusions to the Bible in *The Holy Earth* and *The Seven Stars* suggest that he was schooled in the Christian doctrine.

9. Bailey's comments appeared in an article titled "The Wild Currant, a Sketch," which was published in *College Speculum* in April of 1887; they are quoted in Rodgers, *Bailey* 109.

10. Bailey's textbook, which was in print for decades, was also published under the title *Botany for Secondary Schools*.

11. Norgaard explains that "Positivism is the belief that values and facts can be kept separate. Monism is the belief that the separate sciences—physics, chemistry, biology; the applied sciences such as agriculture, engineering, and forestry; and the social sciences such as economics—lead to a unique answer when confronting complex problems" (*Development Betrayed* 7).

12. *The Apple-Tree* contrasts with another book Bailey wrote early in his life, *Field Notes on Apple Culture* (1886), which is wholly scientific, a manual and guide for apple cultivation. In contrast, *The Apple-Tree* brings together Bailey's comprehensive scientific understanding of the tree with his personal love for it, uniting scientific observation and spiritual experience about the world in his practice of science.

13. Bailey focuses on the relationship between humans and undesirable insects like the codling moth. Such necessary insects as bees, upon which pollination depends, receive little consideration, likely because humans tend not to regard them as pests.

14. Bailey's artful study of the brush pile might also figure as a homage

to the actual art of pruning. J. J. Marois has reminded me that pruning "is a true blending of science and art; skilled workers are paid a very high premium for pruning orchards." Marois, letter to the author, 28 May 1996.

15. The title *The Seven Stars* might itself provide us with Bailey's agenda in the work: it may be an allusion to the Book of Revelations, where John describes a vision of God in which he is directed to write a book and disseminate it; when he faces God, he sees a figure clothed in white, holding seven stars in his right hand (Rev. 1.9–16).

16. Little research has been undertaken about Bailey and his influence on subsequent generations of agrarians and environmentalists. One known link between him and modern environmental thought is Aldo Leopold. Meine has observed that Aldo Leopold read and was influenced by Bailey (see *Aldo Leopold* 214 and 296).

AFTERWORD

1. Bromfield wrote several books during the period of his agricultural experiment. See for example *Pleasant Valley* (1945), *Malabar Farm* (1948), and *Out of the Earth* (1950). For a collection of essays drawn from Bromfield's books dealing with Malabar Farm, see his *Bromfield at Malabar*.

2. Berry is gaining increasing attention among the scholarly community. For a consideration of Berry's attention to nature, see Slovic, *Seeking Awareness*. For an overview of Berry's work see Angyal, *Wendell Berry*.

3. Kittredge has written several books reflecting on how we live and work on the land, including *Owning It All* (1987), *Hole in the Sky* (1992), and *Who Owns the West?* (1996).

WORKS CITED

Ahnebrink, Lars. *The Beginnings of Naturalism in American Fiction*. New York: Russell & Russell, 1961.

Allen, Gay Wilson. *Waldo Emerson: A Biography*. New York: Viking, 1981.

Allen, Gay Wilson, and Roger Asselineau. *An American Farmer: The Life of St. John de Crèvecoeur*. New York: Penguin, 1987.

Angyal, Andrew J. *Wendell Berry*. New York: Twayne, 1995.

Bailey, Liberty Hyde. *The Apple-Tree*. New York: Macmillan, 1922.

———. *Botany: An Elementary Text for Schools*. New York: Macmillan, 1901.

———. *The Country-Life Movement in the United States*. New York: Macmillan, 1911.

———. *The Harvest of the Year to the Tiller of the Soil*. New York: Macmillan, 1927.

———. *The Holy Earth*. New York: Scribner's, 1915.

———. "How the Trees Look in Winter." *Cornell Nature-Study Leaflets and Bulletins*. Leaflet 12. Ithaca, N.Y.: Cornell University, 1904.

———. *The Nature-Study Idea; Being an Interpretation of the New School-Movement to Put the Child in Sympathy with Nature*. New York: Doubleday, Page, 1903.

———. "The Nature-Study Movement." *Cornell Nature-Study Leaflets and Bulletins*. Leaflet 2. Albany, N.Y.: J. B. Lyon, 1904.

———. *The Outlook to Nature*. New York: Macmillan, 1905.

———. "The Science-Spirit in a Democracy." *Ground-Levels in Democracy*. Ithaca, N.Y., 1916. 7–27.

———. *The Seven Stars*. New York: Macmillan, 1923.

———. "What Is Agricultural Education?" *Cornell Nature-Study Leaflets*. Leaflet 4. Albany, N.Y.: J. B. Lyon, 1904.

———. "What Is Nature-Study?" *Cornell Nature-Study Leaflets*. Leaflet 1. Ithaca, N.Y.: Cornell University, 1904.

Becker, George J. "Modern Realism as a Literary Movement." *Documents of Modern Literary Realism*. Ed. George J. Becker. Princeton: Princeton UP, 1963. 3–38.

Berry, Wendell. *The Unsettling of America: Culture and Agriculture*. San Francisco: Sierra Club Books, 1977.

Berthoff, Warner. *The Ferment of Realism: American Literature 1884–1919*. New York: Free, 1965.

Biehl, Janet. *Finding Our Way: Rethinking Ecofeminist Politics*. New York: Black Rose, 1991.

Bookchin, Murray. *The Philosophy of Social Ecology: Essays on Dialectical Naturalism*. Rev. ed. Montreal: Black Rose, 1995.

Bowden, Martyn J. "The Great American Desert and the American Frontier, 1800–1882: Popular Images of the Plains." *Anonymous Americans: Explorations in Nineteenth-Century Social History*. Ed. Tamara K. Harhaven. Englewood Cliffs, N.J.: Prentice-Hall, 1971. 48–79.

Bowers, William L. *The County Life Movement in America, 1900–1920*. Port Washington, N.Y.: Kennikat, 1974.

Bromfield, Louis. *Louis Bromfield at Malabar: Writings on Farming and Country Life*. Ed. Charles E. Little. Baltimore: Johns Hopkins UP, 1988.

Brooks, Paul. *The People of Concord: One Year in the Flowering of New England*. Chester, Conn.: Globe Pequot, 1990.

Brown, Richard D. *Modernization: The Transformation of American Life, 1600–1865*. New York: Hill and Wang, 1976.

Bryant, Edwin. *What I Saw in California*. Lincoln: U of Nebraska P, 1985.

Buell, Lawrence. *The Environmental Imagination: Thoreau, Nature Writing, and the Formation of American Culture*. Cambridge: Belknap Press of Harvard UP, 1995.

Capra, Fritjof. "Systems Theory and the New Paradigm." Merchant, *Ecology* 334–41.

——. *The Turning Point: Science, Society and the Rising Culture*. New York: Bantam, 1982.

Cayton, Mary Kupiec. *Emerson's Emergence: Self and Society in the Transformation of New England, 1800–1845*. Chapel Hill: U of North Carolina P, 1989.

Chase, Richard Volney. *The American Novel and Its Tradition*. Garden City, N.Y.: Doubleday, 1957.

Civello, Paul. *American Literary Naturalism and Its Twentieth-Century Transformations.* Athens: U of Georgia P, 1994.

Cochrane, Willard W. *The Development of American Agriculture: A Historical Analysis.* 2nd ed. Minneapolis: U of Minnesota P, 1993.

Corrington, Roger. "Emerson and the Agricultural Midworld." *Agriculture and Human Values* 7.1 (1990): 20–26.

Country Life Commission. *Report of the Commission on Country Life.* New York: Sturgis & Walton, 1909.

Cowley, Malcolm. "A Natural History of American Naturalism." *Documents of Modern Literary Realism.* Ed. George J. Becker. Princeton: Princeton UP, 1963. 429–51.

Crèvecoeur, J. Hector St. John de. *Letters from an American Farmer; and, Sketches of Eighteenth-Century America.* Ed. Albert E. Stone. New York: Penguin, 1981.

Danbom, David B. *The Resisted Revolution: Urban America and the Industrialization of Agriculture, 1900–1930.* Ames: Iowa State UP, 1979.

Danhof, Clarence H. *Change in Agriculture: The Northern United States, 1820–1870.* Cambridge: Harvard UP, 1969.

Duvall, Bill. "The Deep Ecology Movement." Merchant, *Ecology* 125–39.

Devall, Bill, and George Sessions. *Deep Ecology.* Salt Lake City: Gibbs Smith, 1985.

Diamond, Irene, and Gloria Feman Orenstein, eds. *Reweaving the World: The Emergence of Ecofeminism.* San Francisco: Sierra Club, 1990.

Dillingham, William B. *Frank Norris: Instinct and Art.* Lincoln: U of Nebraska P, 1969.

Dorf, Philip. *Liberty Hyde Bailey: An Informal Biography.* Ithaca, N.Y.: Cornell UP, 1956.

Ehrenfeld, David. *The Arrogance of Humanism.* New York: Oxford UP, 1981.

Ellis, Jeffrey C. "On the Search for a Root Cause: Essentialist Tendencies in Environmental Discourse." *Uncommon Ground: Toward Reinventing Nature.* Ed. William Cronon. New York: Norton, 1995. 256–68.

Emerson, Ralph Waldo. *The Collected Works of Ralph Waldo Emerson.* Ed. Robert E. Spiller and Alfred R. Ferguson. Vol. 1. Cambridge: Belknap Press of Harvard UP, 1971.

——. *The Complete Works of Ralph Waldo Emerson.* 12 vols. New York: AMS, 1979. Reprint of 1903–04 centenary edition published by Houghton Mifflin, Boston.

——. *The Early Lectures of Ralph Waldo Emerson.* Ed. Stephen E.

Whicher, Robert E. Spiller, and Wallace E. Williams. 3 vols. Cambridge: Belknap Press of Harvard UP, 1959–64.

——. *Essays: First and Second Series*. New York: Vintage Books, 1990.

——. *The Journals and Miscellaneous Notebooks of Ralph Waldo Emerson*. 16 vols. Cambridge: Belknap Press of Harvard UP, 1960–82.

——. *Nature. The Complete Essays and Other Writings of Ralph Waldo Emerson*. Ed. Brooks Atkinson. New York: Modern Library, 1940. 1–42.

Evernden, Neil. *The Social Creation of Nature*. Baltimore: Johns Hopkins UP, 1992.

Foucault, Michel. "Of Other Spaces." *Diacritics* 16 (spring 1986): 22–27.

Garland, Hamlin. *Companions on the Trail: A Literary Chronicle*. New York: Macmillan, 1931.

——. *Crumbling Idols*. Cambridge: Belknap Press of Harvard UP, 1960.

——. *Jason Edwards: An Average Man*. New York: Appleton, 1897.

——. *A Little Norsk; Or, Ol' Pap's Flaxen*. New York: Appleton, 1892.

——. *Main-Travelled Roads*. New York: Signet, 1962.

——. *Other Main-Travelled Roads*. New York: Harper, 1910.

——. *A Son of the Middle Border*. New York: Macmillan, 1923.

Gilmore, Michael T. *American Romanticism and the Marketplace*. Chicago: U of Chicago P, 1985.

Graham, Don. *The Fiction of Frank Norris: The Aesthetic Context*. Columbia: U of Missouri P, 1978.

Griswold, A. Whitney. "The Agrarian Democracy of Thomas Jefferson." *American Political Science Review* 40.4 (August 1946): 657–81.

Harrison, Stanley R. "Hamlin Garland and the Double Vision of Naturalism." *The Critical Reception of Hamlin Garland: 1891–1978*. Ed. Charles L. P. Silet, Robert E. Welch, and Richard Boudreau. Troy, N.Y.: Whiston, 1985. 318–28.

Hazard, Lucy Lockwood. *The Frontier in American Literature*. New York: Crowell, 1927.

Hicks, John Donald. *The Populist Revolt: A History of the Farmers' Alliance and the People's Party*. Lincoln: U of Nebraska P, 1961.

Hillel, Daniel. *Out of the Earth: Civilization and the Life of the Soil*. New York: Free, 1991.

Hofstadter, Richard. *The Age of Reform*. New York: Vintage Books, 1955.

Holloway, Jean. *Hamlin Garland: A Biography*. Austin: U of Texas P, 1960.

Horwitz, Howard. *By the Law of Nature: Form and Value in Nineteenth-Century America*. New York: Oxford UP, 1991.

Howard, June. *Form and History in American Literary Naturalism.* Chapel Hill: U of North Carolina P, 1985.

Jackson, Wes. *Becoming Native to This Place.* Washington, D.C.: Counterpoint, 1994.

Jefferson, Thomas. "Draft Constitution for Virginia." *Writings.* New York: Literary Classics of the United States, 1984. 336–45.

———. "Notes on the State of Virginia." *Writings.* New York: Literary Classics of the United States, 1984. 123–325.

———. *The Writings of Thomas Jefferson.* Ed. Andrew A. Lipscomb and Albert E. Bergh. Vol. 16. Washington, D.C.: Thomas Jefferson Memorial Association, 1904. 20 vols.

Jehlen, Myra. *American Incarnation: The Individual, the Nation, and the Continent.* Cambridge: Harvard UP, 1986.

Kaplan, Harold. *Power and Order: Henry Adams and the Naturalist Tradition in American Fiction.* Chicago, U of Chicago P, 1981.

Keller, Evelyn Fox. "Gender and Science." *Discovering Reality: Feminist Perspectives on Epistemology, Metaphysics, Methodology, and Philosophy of Science.* Ed. Sandra Harding and Merrill B. Hintikka. Boston: D. Reidel, 1983. 187–205.

Kolodny, Annette. *The Lay of the Land: Metaphor as Experience and History in American Life and Letters.* Chapel Hill: U of North Carolina P, 1975.

Lee, Brian. *American Fiction 1865–1940.* London: Longman, 1987.

Limerick, Patricia. *Desert Passages.* Albuquerque: U of New Mexico P, 1985.

Logsdon, Gene. *At Nature's Pace: Farming and the American Dream.* New York: Pantheon Books, 1994.

Love, Glen A. "Et in Arcadia Ego: Pastoral Theory Meets Ecocriticism." *Western American Literature* 7.3 (November 1992): 195–207.

Martin, Ronald E. *American Literature and the Universe of Force.* Durham, N.C.: Duke UP, 1981.

Marx, Leo. *The Machine in the Garden: Technology and the Pastoral Ideal in America.* New York: Oxford UP, 1964.

McAleer, John. *Ralph Waldo Emerson: Days of Encounter.* Boston: Little, 1984.

McCullough, Joseph B. *Hamlin Garland.* Boston: Twayne, 1978.

McElrath, Joseph R., Jr. *Frank Norris Revisited.* New York: Twayne, 1992.

McEwan, Barbara. *Thomas Jefferson: Farmer.* Jefferson, N.C.: McFarland, 1991.

McMath, Robert C. *American Populism: A Social History, 1877–1898.* New York: Hill and Wang, 1993.

Meeker, Joseph. *The Comedy of Survival: Studies in Literary Ecology.* New York: Scribner's, 1972.

Meine, Curt. *Aldo Leopold: His Life and Work.* Madison: U of Wisconsin P, 1988.

Merchant, Carolyn. *The Death of Nature.* New York: Harper Collins, 1980.

——, ed. *Ecology.* Atlantic Highlands, N.J.: Humanities, 1994.

Meyer, Roy W. "Hamlin Garland and Midwest Farm Fiction." *A Literary History of the American West.* Fort Worth: Texas Christian UP, 1987. 664–81.

Michaels, Walter Benn. *The Gold Standard and the Logic of Naturalism.* Berkeley: U of California P, 1987.

Mill, John Stuart. "Three Essays on Religion: Nature." *Prose of the Victorian Period.* Ed. William E. Buckler. Boston: Houghton, 1958. 312–42.

Mitchell, Lee Clark. *Determined Fictions: American Literary Naturalism.* New York: Columbia UP, 1989.

Montmarquet, James A. *The Idea of Agrarianism: From Hunter-Gatherer to Agrarian Radical in Western Culture.* Moscow: U of Idaho P, 1989.

Murphy, Virginia Reed. *Across the Plains in the Donner Party.* Golden, Colo.: Outbooks, 1980.

Nabhan, Gary Paul, and Stephen Trimble. *The Geography of Childhood: Why Children Need Wild Places.* Boston: Beacon, 1994.

Naess, Arne. "The Shallow and the Deep, Long-Range Ecology Movement: A Summary." *Inquiry* 16 (1973): 95–100.

Norgaard, Richard B. *Development Betrayed: The End of Progress and a Coevolutionary Revisioning of the Future.* London: Routledge, 1994.

Norris, Frank. *The Letters of Frank Norris.* Ed. Franklin Walker. San Francisco: Book Club of California, 1956.

——. *The Octopus: A Story of California.* New York: New American Library, 1964.

——. "The 'Nature' Revival in Literature." *The Responsibilities of the Novelist.* Garden City, N.Y.: Doubleday, 1903. 137–43.

Oelschlaeger, Max. *The Idea of Wilderness: From Prehistory to the Age of Ecology.* New Haven: Yale UP, 1991.

O'Grady, John P. *Pilgrims to the Wild: Everett Ruess, Henry David Tho-*

reau, *John Muir, Clarence King, Mary Austin*. Salt Lake City: U of Utah P, 1993.

Opie, John. *Ogallala: Water for a Dry Land*. Lincoln: U of Nebraska P, 1993.

Passmore, John. *Man's Responsibility for Nature: Ecological Problems and Western Traditions*. 2nd ed. London: Duckworth, 1980.

Pisani, Donald J. *To Reclaim a Divided West: Water, Law, and Public Policy, 1848–1902*. Albuquerque: U of New Mexico P, 1992.

Pizer, Donald. *Hamlin Garland's Early Work and Career*. Berkeley: U of California P, 1960.

———. "Herbert Spencer and the Genesis of Hamlin Garland's Critical System." *Critical Essays on Hamlin Garland*. Ed. James Nagel. Boston: G. K. Hall, 1982. 208–22.

———. *The Novels of Frank Norris*. Bloomington: Indiana UP, 1966.

———. *Realism and Naturalism in Nineteenth-Century American Literature*. Carbondale: Southern Illinois UP, 1966.

Plant, Judith, ed. *Healing the Wounds: The Promise of Ecofeminism*. Philadelphia: New Society, 1989.

Porter, Carolyn. *Seeing and Being: The Plight of the Participant Observer in Emerson, James, Adams, and Faulkner*. Middletown, Conn.: Wesleyan UP, 1981.

Powell, John Wesley. *Report on the Lands of the Arid Region of the United States*. Ed. Wallace Stegner. Cambridge: Belknap Press of Harvard UP, 1962.

———. "The Water Supplies in the Arid Region." *Irrigation Age* 6.2 (1894): 54–65.

Regis, Pamela. *Describing Early America: Bartram, Jefferson, Crèvecoeur, and the Rhetoric of Natural History*. DeKalb: Northern Illinois UP, 1992.

Robinson, David M. "Community and Utopia in Crèvecoeur's Sketches." *American Literature* 61.1 (1990): 17–31.

Rodgers, Andrew Denny, III. *Liberty Hyde Bailey: A Story of American Plant Sciences*. Princeton: Princeton UP, 1949.

Rothenberg, David. *Hand's End: Technology and the Limits of Nature*. Berkeley: U of California P, 1993.

Rueckert, William. "Literature and Ecology: An Experiment in Ecocriticism." *Iowa Review* 9 (winter 1978): 71–86.

Rusk, Ralph L. *The Life of Ralph Waldo Emerson*. New York: Scribner's, 1949.

Said, Edward W. *The World, the Text, and the Critic*. Cambridge: Harvard UP, 1983.

Sarver, Stephanie. "Environmentalism and Literary Studies." *Rocky Mountain Review of Language and Literature* 49.1 (1995): 106–11.

Schmitt, Peter J. *Back to Nature: The Arcadian Myth in Urban America*. Baltimore: Johns Hopkins UP, 1990.

Scudder, Townsend. *Concord: American Town*. Boston: Little, 1947.

Seltzer, Mark. *Bodies and Machines*. New York: Routledge, 1992.

Sessions, George, ed. *Deep Ecology for the Twenty-First Century*. Boston: Shambhala, 1995.

——. "Ecocentrism and the Anthropocentric Detour." Merchant, *Ecology* 140–51.

Shepard, Paul. *Nature and Madness*. San Francisco: Sierra Club Books, 1982.

——. "A Post-Historic Primitivism." *The Wilderness Condition*. Ed. Max Oelschlaeger. San Francisco: Sierra Club Books, 1992. 40–89.

Slovic, Scott. *Seeking Awareness in American Nature Writing: Henry Thoreau, Annie Dilliard, Edward Abbey, Wendell Berry, Barry Lopez*. Salt Lake City: U of Utah P, 1992.

Smith, Henry Nash. *Virgin Land: The American West as Symbol and Myth*. Cambridge: Harvard UP, 1978.

Smythe, Harriet B. "Biographical Sketch." *Irrigation Age* 14.1 (1899): 3–5.

Smythe, William Ellsworth. *The Conquest of Arid America*. New York: Harper, 1900.

——. *The Conquest of Arid America*. 1905. Seattle: U of Washington P, 1969.

——. "The Republic of Irrigation." *Irrigation Age* 6.5 (1894): 189–95.

Snyder, Gary. *The Practice of the Wild*. San Francisco: North Point, 1990.

Steiner, Dieter. "Human Ecology as Transdisciplinary Science, and Science as Part of Human Ecology." *Human Ecology: Fragments of Anti-Fragmentary Views of the World*. Ed. Dieter Steiner and Markus Nauser. New York: Routledge, 1993. 47–76.

Stewart, Edgar I. *Penny-an-Acre Empire in the West*. Norman: U of Oklahoma P, 1968.

Thompson, Paul B. *The Spirit of the Soil: Agriculture and Environmental Ethics*. New York: Routledge, 1995.

Thoreau, Henry David. *Walden, or, Life in the Woods*. New York: New American Library, 1960.

Turner, Frederick Jackson. *The Frontier in American History*. Tucson: U of Arizona P, 1986.

———. "The Problem of the West." *The Frontier in American History*. Tucson: U of Arizona P, 1986. 205–21.

Van Dyke, John C. *The Desert: Further Studies in Natural Appearances*. New York: Scribner's, 1901.

Van Leer, David. *Emerson's Epistemology: The Argument of the Essays*. Cambridge: Cambridge UP, 1986.

Veblen, Thorstein. *Absentee Ownership and Business Enterprise in Recent Times*. New York: B. W. Huebsch, 1923.

Walcutt, Charles C. *American Literary Naturalism: A Divided Stream*. Minneapolis: U of Minnesota P, 1956.

Walker, Franklin. *Frank Norris: A Biography*. Garden City, N.Y.: Doubleday, 1932.

Wall, Joseph Frazier, ed. *The Andrew Carnegie Reader*. Pittsburgh: U of Pittsburgh P, 1992.

Warren, Karen J. "The Power and the Promise of Ecological Feminism." *Environmental Ethics* 12 (1990): 125–46.

White, Hayden. *The Content of the Form: Narrative Discourse and Historical Representation*. Baltimore: Johns Hopkins UP, 1987.

White, Lynn, Jr. "The Historical Roots of Our Ecologic Crisis." *Science* 155 (10 March 1967): 1203–07.

"William Ellsworth Smythe." *National Cyclopedia of American Biography*. 1927 ed.

Wilson, Edward O. *Biophilia*. Cambridge: Harvard UP, 1984.

Worster, Donald. *Nature's Economy*. 2nd ed. Cambridge: Cambridge UP, 1994.

———. *Rivers of Empire: Water, Aridity, and the Growth of the American West*. New York: Oxford UP, 1985.

Wyatt, David. *The Fall into Eden: Landscape and Imagination in California*. Cambridge: Cambridge UP, 1986.

Ziff, Larzer. "Crushed Yet Complacent: Hamlin Garland." *The Critical Reception of Hamlin Garland: 1891–1978*. Ed. Charles L. P. Silet, Robert E. Welch, and Richard Boudreau. Troy, N.Y.: Whitston, 1985. 282–95.

Zimmerman, Michael. *Contesting Earth's Future: Radical Ecology and Postmodernity*. Berkeley: U of California P, 1994.

INDEX

farmers (*continued*)
36, 53–54, 64–65, 69–74; as naturalists, 13; New England, 36–37, 39;
relationship with nature, 13–14,
15–16; Smythe on arid lands and,
119–23; yeoman, 179 n.6

farmer stewardship: historic lineage
of, 176 n.16; over nature, 33; political complex of, 34

farm families: Garland's depiction of,
54–55, 58, 59–60; Norris's depiction of, 91; relationship between
farm and, 40–41

farming: Bailey on business of, 163–
64; Bailey on society and, 145–
46, 150–53; as connection to nonhuman nature, 16–17, 73; economic
realities of, 13; Emerson's model of,
31–43; as form of education, 25–26;
Garland on economics of, 53, 58–
64, 70–73; Garland on individuals
effected by, 50–51; Garland's vision
of, 51–52, 58–59; Norris on economics of, 75–76, 81–83, 89–92,
93–95, 96; technology of, 96–97.
See also agriculture

"Farming" (Emerson address): definition of nature in, 21–22, 28–30;
rhetorical inconsistencies in, 18, 53;
on tension of nature and culture,
31–32, 45; on unsettled lands, 16;
view of farm/farming in, 20–21,
27, 31–43

farming metaphors, 3, 23–24, 27. *See
also* metaphors

farm management debates, 182 n.15

farms: Bailey on democracy and family, 133–34; Bailey on increase of
corporate, 150, 152–53; Brook Farm
community, 38–39; Emerson's doctrine of the, 26, 30–31, 175 n.9;
failure due to nature, 63–64;
"Farming" (Emerson) view of, 20–
21, 27, 28–29, 37–43; intellec-
tual/spiritual inquiry through, 26;

Jefferson's promotion of the, 11–13;
as metaphoric vehicle, 3, 23–24, 27;
relationship between family and,
40–41; Smythe's vision of small
communities of, 131

feminine nature, 41–42, 44

Field, Forest and Garden Botany
(Gray), 134

Foucault, Michel, 29

Fuller, Margaret, 38

Garland, Hamlin: affection for land
by, 47–49, 51; agrarian literature
of, 2, 3, 12, 17; "Among the Corn
Rows," 59, 60, 64, 65–67; background of, 46–47; Bailey compared
to, 136; *Boy Life on the Prairie*, 51,
73; career phases of, 179 n.5; compared to Bailey, 164; compared to
Smythe, 131; *Crumbling Idols*, 49–
50, 57, 74; "A Day's Pleasure," 59;
depiction of farm families by, 54–
55, 58, 59–60; dual vision of farm
life by, 51–52, 58–59; "God's
Ravens," 68–69; on inherent goodness, 68–69; interpretation of nature by, 52–53; on isolation of farm
women, 126; *Jason Edwards*, 61, 63,
64, 72; literary focus of, 56–57; *A
Little Norsk*, 62, 64, 67–68; "Local
Color in Art," 49–50; "Lucretia
Burns," 57–58, 59, 61, 66–67;
Main-Travelled Roads, 17, 47, 50–
51, 57, 167; "New Fields," 50; *Other
Main-Travelled Roads*, 51, 57; pastoral sensibility of, 7; *Prairie Folks*,
17, 51, 57; realistic literature of, 53–
54, 64–65, 69–74; "The Return of
the Private," 69; romanticism of
works by, 180 n.12; as single-tax
social reformer, 62, 180 n.11; *A Son of
the Middle Border*, 47–48; stylistic
irony of, 70–71; "Under the Lion's
Paw," 60–61, 62, 69, 73; "Up the
Coulee," 59, 60, 64, 65

Judeo-Christian tradition and view of, 8, 141–43, 187 n.7; manifold meanings of, 9–10, 176 n.10; masculine farmer and feminine, 41–42, 44; mechanistic interpretations of, 43–44; nonhuman, 10, 16–17, 73; Norris on relationships of humans to, 85–91; prehistoric man's closeness to, 173 n.5; relationship of farmers to, 13–14, 15–16; technology and understanding, 82–83, 181 n.9; tension between culture and, 31–32, 45; wildness and, 8–9, 174 n.9. *See also* land; nonhuman environments

Nature (Emerson): meaning of, 175 n.2; on nature as commodity, 44–45; on purpose of nature, 26; theory of nature in, 21–22, 28–30

nature poetry, 140

"The 'Nature' Revival in Literature" (Norris), 101

nature study, 138–39, 140

The Nature-Study Idea (Bailey), 137, 141–42

"The Nature-Study Movement" (Bailey), 138–39

nature writing, 6–7, 183 n.20

New England farmers: changing practices of, 36–37; diminished economic returns of, 39

"New Fields" (Garland), 50

New Paradigm (Zimmerman), 128

nonhuman environments: Bailey's work on, 136–41, 144, 148–49; "Farming" (Emerson) on, 35–36; history to examine human and, 41; human relationships with, 5; individualistic view of, 30–31; literature about, 52; nineteenth-century depictions of, 55–56; Norris on human relationship to, 85–102; Norris's exclusion of, 78–79. *See also* human relationships; nature; technology

nonhuman nature: described, 10; farming as connection to, 16–17, 73. *See also* nature

Norris, Frank: agricultural transformation documented by, 3; books by, 2; compared to Smythe, 131; *McTeague*, 79; naturalist philosophy of, 54; "The 'Nature' Revival in Literature," 101; philosophy of, 182 n.10; on plans to write epic, 75–76. See also *The Octopus* (Norris)

Northern Pacific Railroad, 109

"Notes on the State of Virginia" (Jefferson), 11–12

octopus metaphor, 80–81, 90, 94–95

The Octopus (Norris): agricultural/political themes of, 80–85; character studies within, 79; on human and nonhuman relationships, 85–102; inaccuracies within, 77–78, 181 n.5; irrigation ditch in, 84–85; metaphors used in, 80–85; naturalist ethics of, 61; on Norris's plans to write, 75–76; Norris's process of writing, 77–78; plot of, 17–18, 76–77; rhetorical inconsistency in, 53, 103; on social/political contexts of agriculture, 79–80, 168. *See also* Norris, Frank

Oelschlaeger, Max, 7

"One Crop Error in the West" (Smythe), 128–29

On the Origin of Species by Means of Natural Selection (Darwin), 134

O Pioneers! (Cather), 167

Other Main-Travelled Roads (Garland), 51, 57

Our Barren Lands pamphlet (Hazen), 109

Overland Monthly, 101

Parkman, Francis, 109

pastoralism, 5–7; American fantasy of, 5–6; Bailey and, 7, 161; Emerson

society: Bailey on farming impact on, 145–46, 150–53; individual/environment and, 44–45, 72–73; Smythe's vision of American West, 123–26; technology and loss of values by, 159. *See also* culture

A Son of the Middle Border (Garland), 47–48

spiritual regeneration, 66–68

Steinbeck, John: agrarian literature of, 3, 4; *The Grapes of Wrath*, 168

stewardship model, 33, 34, 176 n.16

Stewart, Edgar I., 109

Taine, Hippolyte, 49, 54

Talks Afield: About Plants and the Science of Plants (Bailey), 135

technology: conceptions of nature and role of, 181 n.9; within farming, 96–97; as nature, 82–83; octopus metaphor as beyond, 94; plow, 177 n.19; relationships of human, 102; and societal loss of values, 159. *See also* nonhuman environments; science

Thompson, Paul B., 33

Thoreau, Henry David, 3, 6, 7

A Thousand Acres (Smiley), 171

Three Farms (Kramer), 170

tropes, 114–15

"Under the Lion's Paw" (Garland), 60–61, 62, 69, 73

Unsettling of America (Berry), 169

"Up the Coulee" (Garland), 59, 60, 64, 65

"The Uses of Natural History" (Emerson), 23–24, 30–31

Van Dyke, John C., 112

Walcutt, Charles, 55

Walker, Franklin, 76

Walker, Mildred, *Winter Wheat*, 167–68

water debates, 110–11

What Is Agricultural Education? (Bailey), 146

wheat metaphor, 80–81, 83–84, 93, 98

White, Gilbert, 23, 24

White, Lynn, Jr., 8

wildness, 8–9, 174 n.9

Wind and Weather (Bailey), 158

Winter Wheat (Walker), 167–68

women: agrarian literature by, 4; consumer culture and, 160; ecofeminism on, 44, 178 n.25; elision from agrarian economy of, 42; Garland on misery of farm, 60; isolation of farm, 126, 185 n.14; spiritual rejuvenation through nature of, 67. *See also* Cather, Willa; Hasselstrom, Linda; Smiley, Jane; Walker, Mildred

Worster, Donald, 127

Wright, Harry M., 75, 76

yeoman farmer, 11, 16, 22, 51, 58, 68, 69, 70, 71, 179 n.6 n.10

"The Young American" (Emerson), 38–39

Young, Brigham, 108

Zimmerman, Michael, 128